As a grandfather of six, I highly recommend Grandparenting Through Obstacles *to every grandparent. I cannot remember a time when the role that grandparents play in the lives of their grandchildren has been more desperately needed. This book is an essential resource to help in that endeavor. The use of true, heartfelt stories to convey a message and model Christ-like solutions is powerful. This book will bless you and help you to become more effective in the lives of those little ones whom you love.*

Jim Ertel, Founder
Heart of the Family Ministries
www.heartofthefamily.org

Practical suggestions, inspiring prayers, and real-life experiences from today's grandparents make this book a 'must-read' for any grandmother and grandfather who want to share Christ with their grandchildren, but face obstacles from family members who disagree with Christian beliefs or who are resistant to any influence but their own. Help and hope are here!

Karen O'Connor, Author
Innovative Grandparenting
Grandkids Say the Cutest Things
Bein' a Grandparent Ain't For Wimps

Grandparenting Through Obstacles *by Renée Gray-Wilburn and Dianne E. Butts is a refreshing and practical approach to the common issues of grandparenting that many of us, as Christians, have encountered. I am a grandmother many times over, and even a great-grandmother now, but I can say wholeheartedly that this book has helped me with issues I've grappled over for years. Thank you, Renée and Dianne, for writing with such poignant wisdom. This book is a true blessing indeed!*

Kathi Macias, Author
The Deliverer **and** ***Unexpected Christmas Hero***
www.kathimacias.com

Three cheers for Grandparenting Through Obstacles. *One of the most difficult challenges in life is having a strong desire to influence your grandchildren in a positive way and having the parents oppose you. This book gives great hope and practical advice to Christian grandparents who face this challenge.*

Christine Crosby, Editorial Director
GRAND – The Online Magazine for GRANDparents
www.GrandMagazine.com

Renée Gray-Wilburn and Dianne E. Butts have crafted a book for grandparents that is inspiring, practical, and fun. The compilation of grandparenting stories runs the gamut from typical scenarios to non-traditional situations such as grandparenting foster children or grandchildren who are ill. They offer practical suggestions at the end of each chapter, resources and ideas, Scripture, questions to ponder and prayers. It is the most complete book for Christian grandparenting I have run across. It is easy to read and would make a welcome addition to any grandparent's library.

Golden Keyes Parsons
Historical fiction author
Eight grandchildren and four great-grandchildren

Grandparenting Through Obstacles, *by Renée Gray-Wilburn and Dianne E. Butts, provides an excellent resource for grandparents today, who wish to provide a godly example to their grandkids. Some of the challenges they face are parents not walking with the Lord, families being far away—either across the country or around the world—and non-traditional families. This book is filled with true stories of grandparents who have faced these challenges and learned ways to partner with their children to love and encourage their grandchildren and to teach them to own their own faith.*

Susan Titus Osborn
Director, TCC Manuscript Critique Service
Author of 30 books

Grandparenting Through Obstacles

Overcoming Family Challenges to Reach Your Grandchildren for Christ

Renée Gray-Wilburn

Dianne E. Butts

PNP

ISBN-13: 978-1-938092-17-6
ISBN-10: 1938092171

Published by Pix-N-Pens Publishing, 130 Prominence Point Pkwy. #130-330, Canton, GA 30114, www.PixNPens.com

To order additional copies of this resource online, visit www.PixNPens.com.

Printed in the United States of America.

FOREWORD

It is true that few things are grander than being a grandparent. It's also true that at times few things can be more challenging than being a grandparent. Grandparenting today is often anything but what we expect it to be.

I became a grandfather for the first time on June 1, 1997. It was a day I will never forget. As I held my first grandchild, a flood of emotions spilled over me. The first was the joy of holding my grandson—a second generation now living with my DNA. There was also the shocking realization that I had now become a full-fledge member of an elite class—albeit a class marked by gray hair and a label I had hitherto only applied to "old" people. Was it really possible I could now be a grandfather?

As real as these emotions were, one emotion erupted within me unexpectedly. It was the sudden awareness of the kind of world my generation was leaving for our grandchildren to navigate as they grew. The epitaph of the generation that immediately followed Joshua and his generation came to mind. It read as follows: "Another generation grew up, who knew neither the Lord nor what He had done ..." (Judges 2:10). I resolved at that moment to do whatever God gave me to do to make sure my grandson would know the Lord and the wondrous grace He has lavished on us through the Cross.

Little did I understand the challenges involved in that task that lay ahead.

Renée and Dianne understand that grandparenting in today's world is very different from what it was only one generation ago. Numerous obstacles—from raising grandchildren to long-distance grandparenting—face many grandparents today. More than that, grandparents must deal with the effects upon our families caused by widespread divorce, strained family relationships, increased godlessness and a culture hostile to absolute truth. How do we face these challenges and help guide these next generations towards an authentic, wholehearted faith in Jesus Christ?

The authors have assembled a collage of life stories from grandparents who live where you live and know what you are facing. These stories will encourage you, stir you, and inspire you in your own journey. Above all, these stories will fill your grandparenting toolbox with some exciting new tools that will impact your own grandchildren and families with the reality of the Gospel.

These stories reveal the vital and important role of grandparents to intentionally mentor and model Christ-likeness among our grandchildren. It is incumbent upon us to make sure our life makes Christ look great so that they too would want to submit to Him and follow Him with all their heart. Obviously, this is best accomplished in partnership with the parents of our grandchildren, and by linking of arms with other grandparents who share our passion to live for the next generations.

I pray this book of real-life stories will give you hope and stay your resolve to remain steadfast in this grand calling we call grandparenting. May the stories of God's goodness and the faithful intentionality of these grandparents' stories keep you from losing heart in the face of whatever obstacles are encountered in your own story. Perhaps your story will one day be added to these you now hold so that the legacy can continue.

Cavin T. Harper
Executive Director
Christian Grandparenting Network
Author, *Not on Our Watch:*
Courageous Grandparenting in a Turbulent World

www.christiangrandparenting.net

TABLE OF CONTENTS

*pseudonym

Introduction

It's a grand time of life! Ever since your own children grew up, you've look forward to having grandchildren. You've dreamt of the fun things you'll do with them and the ways you'll enjoy them and spoil them. You've looked forward to watching them grow in every way.

You watched as your first grandchild was added to the family. Maybe you're blessed to have more than one now. Perhaps they're still little. Or maybe they're already teenagers.

It was a grand dream, and now you're living it! And there's so much you want to share with your grandchildren—your love, family memories, and most importantly, your Christian faith.

But there's a snag. Not everything is as grand as you dreamed it would be. You've run into challenges as a grandparent that you never expected:

- Your child isn't walking with God, which creates many unforeseen challenges in sharing your faith with your grandchildren;
- Your children live far away, and you're trying to build relationships with your grandchildren long distance;
- Your child is divorced or otherwise a single parent, and you're having to carry the load of helping raise your grandchildren; or,

- You simply need to figure out how to establish a successful partnership with your children when it comes to your grandchildren.

Perhaps your grandparenting dream hasn't been as easy as you may have once thought. The good news is that you're not alone. Today, nearly one-third of all adults in the United States are grandparents.[1] Many of these are Christians, who, like yourself, desire to reach their grandchildren for Christ. The burden on Christian grandparents today is greater than ever as they provide a crucial link to winning a generation to Jesus.

The number of Americans who identify themselves as Christians is steadily declining with each generation. According to a 2007 Barna Group report, of those Americans 61 years of age and older, 77 percent identify themselves as Christian; of those 42 to 50 years old (many of whom are already grandparents), 73 percent do. But for younger generations of Americans (16 to 29 years old), only 60 percent identify themselves as Christians.[2] Another study shows that, of this current generation of children born since 1984, only 4 percent say they regularly attend church and believe the Bible.[3] Because worldview is primarily shaped by the time children turn thirteen,[4] teaching kids a Christian worldview early in their lives is critical to their spiritual formation.

---

[1] eds., "Surprising Facts about Grandparents," Grandparents.com, August 12, 2009, http://bit.ly/KtbPEB.

[2] "A New Generation Expresses Its Skepticism and Frustration with Christianity," *The Barna Update*, August 24, 2007.

[3] Thom S. Rainer, *The Bridger Generation* (Nashville, TN: Broadman & Holman, 2006).

[4] "Barna Survey Examines Changes in Worldview Among Christians over the Past 13 Years," *The Barna Update*, March 6, 2009.

Possibly the most troubling news is that more and more younger non-Christians perceive Christianity in a negative way.[5] Therefore, it's likely that your grandchildren's friends and classmates will only serve to undermine the spiritual values you've tried to impart. Receiving godly influence from their family will be an important step in your grandchildren's spiritual growth.

So, how can you successfully influence your grandkids when faced with obstacles within your own family? That's what this book is all about! In each chapter, we'll explore the true story of a real grandparent who is facing the very challenges you may be facing right now and see how that grandparent was able to meet and overcome those challenges to produce spiritual fruit in their grandkids' lives. We'll discuss the lessons found in that story and discover practical applications and fresh ideas you can use to overcome the obstacles of trying to spiritually impact your grandkids. We'll also lead you in some questions—which can be used individually or with a group of grandparenting friends—to help you reflect on your unique situation and find creative solutions. Together we'll pray suggested prayers, read Scripture verses for study and encouragement, learn about grandparents in the Bible, and discover fun tips and resources that will help you with your grandparenting journey. We'll do all we can to empower you to overcome the challenges so you can effectively influence your grandchildren for Christ. And, who knows the impact just one grandchild—perhaps *your* grandchild—may have on a generation.

---

[5] "A New Generation Expresses Its Skepticism and Frustration with Christianity," Barna Group, September 24, 2007, Barna.org. http://bit.ly/LfrIhO

Part 1

The Challenge of Parents
Not Walking with God

Perhaps you became a Christian later in life; therefore, your child did not grow up in a Christian home. Or, maybe your child married a non-believer who slowly caused him to drift from God. Or, it could be your child had a bad experience with another Christian or church and has turned from God because of hurt and bitterness. Whatever the cause, you've found yourself in a situation where your adult child currently does not walk with the Lord.

As difficult as it is for Christian parents to contend for their child's salvation, it turns even harder when those parents become grandparents. You cannot bear to see your grandchild not raised according to biblical values or taught God's Word. It hurts to watch them swept away by a non-Christian culture tide, knowing that without God's Spirit they have few tools to fight it. The current decline in Christianity among upcoming generations concerns you deeply, and you don't want *your* grandchild to become part of that statistic.

How you long to take your grandchild to church with you, to teach her Christian hymns, and read Bible stories to her. In fact, you've probably envisioned such moments long before you ever became a grandparent. You've dreamed of all the ways you wanted to help your grandchild become strong in her faith. If you only had the opportunity to teach her about the Lord and show her what it means to have a relationship with Jesus, you know one day she would make a commitment to follow Him forever.

But now you're wondering how you can possibly do that. You might live right next door to her, but her parents—your child and in-law—do not want you influencing her for Christ. You don't want to do anything that would cause division in your relationship with your child and grandchild, and you don't want to overstep your boundaries as a grandparent. Then again, how do you even define those boundaries when it comes to spiritual matters?

On one hand, your first allegiance should be to God and His Word, which tells you to "make disciples of all nations" (Matthew 28:19). Surely that applies to your own family! But at the same time, Paul tells us, "If it is possible, as far as it depends on you, live at peace with everyone" (Romans 12:18). How do you strike the necessary balance yet retain your family relationships and your sanity?

In Part 1, you'll discover creative ideas and truths from God's Word to help you attain this balance. The grandparents in the stories that follow all had unique challenges they had to conquer to reach their grandkids spiritually when their own children were not walking with God.

In one case, a grandmother had a daughter who was not walking with God and whose family literally lived on the other side of the world, making it especially difficult for Grandma to have quality conversations about Jesus with her grandchildren. In another story, the grandparent had to maneuver around the obstacle of an alcoholic child to reach her grandchild, who desperately needed Grandma's attention and moral input. Other stories include a four-year-old who comes to live with Grandma after her parents both relapse into drug abuse, parents who simply have no interest in a spiritual upbringing for their child, and a granddaughter who remembers her grandmother's constant whispering of prayers that taught her to pray through her parent's tumultuous marriage and divorce and beyond to her own marriage.

Through each of these challenges, God answered their calls for help. He gave them ideas, helped them persevere through prayer, and taught them how to apply biblical principles to their family relationships. They learned a lot through their struggles and their walk of faith, and you will, too.

Whatever circumstances you're facing with your child and grandchild, God will help you understand how to apply the lessons these grandparents learned to your own situation. You'll be encouraged. What God did for these grandparents, He can do for you, too (Acts 10:34)!

Chapter 1

The Power of Prayer, Love, and a Secret Agent
by Marilyn Stouter*

Jennifer burst through my bedroom door one peaceful Sunday morning as I dressed for church. "Stop filling my children's heads with your crazy stories you claim are true because they're from the Bible. If you don't I can assure you that my family will not be visiting you again."

I stood dumbfounded, totally shocked by my daughter's outburst. I said the first thing that came to mind. "What was I supposed to tell Lindsey? When a child asks me a question, I need to respond the best I know how. She asked a question about God, and I told her what I knew from what the Bible says." We stared at each other in silence for what seemed like several minutes before Jennifer turned on her heels and marched out the door.

My mind immediately flashed back to a similar incident a few years prior when Jennifer and her family visited me in Seattle from their home in the Philippines. Her children, Lindsey and Ryan, who then were only six and five, respectively, asked if they could watch the *Jesus* movie on video. I had no sooner popped the tape into the VCR, and Jennifer came downstairs and asked what we were watching. In her excitement, Lindsey announced, "The movie about Jesus!" Jennifer said no, they could not watch that movie. Amidst Lindsey's and Ryan's protests, I explained that we needed to follow

Mommy's rules and watch something else. Today, I felt my heart ache for them all over again just as I did that day.

There was a time Jennifer sought God, but over the years, she's drifted away and become skeptical of all things Christian. Becoming a Christian myself late in life, Jennifer was not brought up knowing about Jesus. It's particularly hard to reach her now because of the overseas miles between us.

I've always determined not to give up on my children's or grandchildren's salvation, knowing there's no distance in the spirit. I know my prayers can affect them no matter how far apart we live. Often, my only recourse is prayer since I'm not allowed to speak freely to my grandchildren about God when their mother is around. I learned a long time ago that preaching to Jennifer only drives her further away. I believe my job is to love her and God's is to bring her into His kingdom.

> ### *Alone Time Idea*
>
> *Find a special place that you can visit with your grandkids—maybe a park, a beach, or even the garden in your backyard. Make this your regular "alone time getaway" where you can go without distractions to talk about their lives, your family, and God.*

Jennifer's threat that day of never visiting again hit hard. To be so far away and not permitted to see my family would be devastating.

Shaken, I continued dressing for church and left my house in silence. I tried to engage in our church's praise and worship, but my mind remained in my bedroom, reliving the showdown with my daughter. But God stirred my heart, and I felt strongly that I needed to return home. When I opened the door, Jennifer turned from washing dishes.

"What brings you home?"

"I came to apologize," I said. "I love you very much, and I would never do anything to come between you and your children. I hope you can forgive me."

Jennifer dried her hands and threw her arms around me. I returned to church filled with God's peace.

Something happened that day in my daughter. I believe the power of God's love, released through my apology, began working to soften her heart. Soon, she allowed me to take my grandchildren with me to church, which I relished. Oddly enough, it wasn't the time at church that affected my grandkids as much as it was our time in the car driving there and back. God used that time with just the three of us to help me plant kingdom seeds.

One way I've always prayed for my grandchildren is that God would give them a spiritual hunger. He certainly answered that

An Encouraging Word

"Grandparents are a family's greatest treasure, the founders of a loving legacy, the greatest storytellers, the keepers of traditions that linger on in cherished memory. Grandparents are the family's strong foundation. Their very special love sets them apart. Through happiness and sorrow, through their special love and caring, grandparents keep a family close at heart."
(author unknown)

prayer. As we drove, Lindsey and Ryan constantly fired questions at me.

"Grandma, how come God never speaks to me?" eight-year-old Lindsey asked one morning on the way to church.

"Well, He does speak to us—all the time. But sometimes we just don't know how to listen. It takes practice to learn to hear God's voice. Ask Him again to talk to you and trust that He will. I think you'll be surprised."

When I picked the kids up from their service that morning, Lindsey beamed. "Grandma! It worked! God spoke to me at church."

"Really?" I asked. "What did He say?"

"He said He loves me."

"Yep, that sounds like God," I replied.

"Grandma, for the first time I really know that God loves me."

Another way I've prayed for my grandkids is for God to send other believers into their lives to influence them for Christ.

God miraculously answered this prayer by giving my daughter and son-in-law a Christian nanny. Because Jennifer and her husband both work, they needed someone to help with the kids. They hired a live-in nanny, who they didn't realize was a Christian. I call Susanne my "secret agent" because she regularly updates me on the children and tells how she discreetly ministers to them about the Lord. Susanne always travels with the family, including their visits to Washington to see me. Through her witness, God provides a way for my grandchildren to learn how to apply biblical truths to their daily lives—something I can't do because of the distance.

Even at their current ages of nine and ten, my grandchildren have grown tremendously in the Lord. When we're together, they often express concern over their parents not knowing Jesus. I tell them not to worry, because if God can touch their own hearts in spite of living in a non-Christian home, He can certainly reach their parents now that Jesus' light is shining through them.

I encourage my grandchildren not to talk much about Jesus to their mom and dad because I know it won't be received, but instead to just pray for them.

"Grandma, since we're on the same team, can we pray for Mom and Dad together?" Ryan asked one day.

"Absolutely," I said. The three of us prayed right then that God would use them in a special way to reach their parents.

Through years of prayer, planting seeds of God's truth and love during whatever snippets of time I have alone with my grandkids, and the influence of other Christians in my grandchildren's lives, God has incredibly captured Lindsey's and Ryan's hearts —in spite of their parents' roadblocks.

Knowing how God cherishes children's prayers, now that my grandchildren are on my "team," I'm certain it's just a matter of time before our prayers of salvation for my daughter and son-in-law are answered.

Grandparents in the Bible

Abraham and Sarah: Grandparents of Jacob-Israel

Abraham and Sarah were the parents of Isaac and the grandparents of Esau and Jacob-Israel. Although Esau and Jacob spent most of their lives quarreling, Jacob is the father of the twelve tribes of Israel. After Jacob wrestled with the holy Visitor at Peniel, God changed his name to Israel (Genesis 32:28), which means, "he struggles with God." Yet, Jacob-Israel is the father of, and bequeathed his new name to, God's beloved people.

God made promises to Abraham that would ultimately bless all people. He is able to keep His promises regardless of quarreling, family dynamics, or an individual's choice to walk with Him or not.

Points to Ponder

> ➢ What are the different ways that Grandma mentioned she prayed for her grandchildren? How can you apply these prayers to your own situation?

> ➢ Consider Grandma's response to Jennifer's reaction over both the *Jesus* movie and Lindsey's question. What lessons can you apply to your situation regarding her response?

> ➢ What do you think of Grandma's comment, "I believe my job is to love her and God's is to bring her into His kingdom"? What are some ways you can love your children or grandchildren into His kingdom?

> ➢ What do you find hard about just doing your part then allowing God to do His part when it comes to your family's salvation?

> ➢ What do you think about Grandma's statement: "I encourage my grandchildren not to talk much about Jesus to their mom and dad"? When might it be wise to not share about Jesus?

Steps to Take

1. Ask God to show you areas where you may need to ask forgiveness from your child in regards to your relationship with your grandchildren. Allow God to direct you in the steps to take with your child to reconcile any differences in your relationship.

2. Start a new tradition with your grandkids of having a special alone time with them when you're together. Make it a time of fun activities, yet also a time for planting kingdom seeds into their hearts.

3. Ask God to lead you in practical and tangible ways of expressing His love to your grandchildren and their parents. How can you be Christ to them simply through your actions?

Scriptures to Study

"I am sending you out like sheep among wolves. Therefore be as shrewd as snakes and as innocent as doves" (Matthew 10:16).

❖ Sometimes dealing with family members can seem as though we are being thrown to the wolves! The grandmother in this story acted with shrewdness and wisdom, yet also innocence when responding to Jennifer, who was not always cooperative.

In what ways might you need to find a balance between being shrewd and innocent in trying to work with your child concerning your grandkids?

"Above all, love each other deeply, because love covers over a multitude of sins" (1 Peter 4:8).

❖ Although this grandmother didn't do anything wrong, she apologized to Jennifer for any hurt her daughter may have felt as a result of the grandmother's interactions with Lindsey and Ryan. By choosing to walk in love with her daughter, God was able to soften Jennifer's heart.

What are some areas where you may have to choose to walk in love with your child even though you may not be doing anything wrong?

"It's not important who does the planting, or who does the watering. What's important is that God makes the seed grow" (1 Cor. 3:7, NLT).

❖ This grandma understood that hers was only one part of the total process of reaching her grandkids and that it doesn't matter who God uses to plant or water His seeds. Ultimately, He is the one responsible for their spiritual growth.

Are you having difficulty allowing God to do only what He can do? Ask Him to help you understand better what your role is in your grandchildren's spiritual journey.

One Way to Pray

Dear Lord, show me how I can strengthen my relationship with my children and grandchildren through the power of Your love. Give me ideas of practical ways to let them know how much You care about them and love them. Help me also to walk in forgiveness toward my family and to ask for forgiveness when I hurt them in any way. I ask You to send other Christians into my children's and grandchildren's lives who will also display Your love to them and lead them closer to You. Thank You for filling their hearts with a desire to know You and for revealing Your love to them. In Jesus' name. Amen.

Prayers, Notes, or Ideas

_____

_____

_____

_____

_____

_____

_____

_____

_____

_____

Chapter 2

A Divine Role in God's Theater
by Elaine Burbridge

I couldn't help but hear my thirteen-year-old granddaughter, Kelsey, emphatically repeat into her cell phone, "Mama, you don't have to come home. It's really okay. You don't have to hurry." As I listened to Kelsey's voice fill with disappointment, I wanted to scream, "Who's the real grown-up here, my middle-aged daughter or my teenage granddaughter?" How I wanted to grab that phone and tell my daughter a thing or two!

Kelsey had planned to spend the night with me, but when I picked her up that afternoon, she explained that she and her mother had to work on her birthday party plans. They'd decided to do so that evening, so she wouldn't be able to spend the night after all. I was disappointed, but I knew the party plans were more important.

I suggested to Kelsey, "Let's just grab a quick bite to eat instead. Then I'll take you home so you can get to work."

On the way to lunch, Kelsey's excitement made me laugh as she told me her birthday wishes. I watched the joy spill across her face. "I want a new party dress. And I want to go to a nice restaurant with a bunch of my friends, and then get a limousine to drive us all over town!"

I remember thinking how that did sound like loads of fun. Then abruptly I was brought back to the painful present upon hearing Kelsey's repeated conciliatory statements: "Mama, it's really okay if we don't talk about my birthday party tonight. Please, just stay at your friend's house. Don't try to drive. Be safe. I love you."

I couldn't believe my daughter, Caren's, behavior. Her alcohol addiction had prevented her from enjoying many special times with Kelsey. And here was one more of those special times ruined.

I try not to jeopardize my relationship with my daughter by acting better than her or by pointing an accusatory finger in her direction. I've often wished I could keep her from hurting herself, but I realized long ago it wasn't something I could do, no matter how much I loved her.

Her addiction to alcohol and cigarettes began at age sixteen. Now at forty, she's fallen prey to her addictions' promises of peace and comfort, as fleeting as those sensations always are.

But, as Kelsey's grandmother, I believe there are some things I can do to protect her from the pain my daughter causes. The best protection, I've found, is staying as physically and emotionally close to her as possible. I even learned to send text messages from my cell phone so she and I would be only a text away.

I also frequently invite her to do things I know she loves. "C'mon, Kelsey, let's go shopping," I'll call and announce unexpectedly. Or, "If you're not doing anything Saturday night, I'll take you to the movies." She's always quick to accept my invitations to get out of her house for a while.

I love spending fun times with my granddaughter, but more importantly, these outings offer me an opportunity to subtly influence her choices, which, left to her own judgments, often aren't so good. When we shop, we talk about dressing appropriately and what Jesus must think of some of the clothes teens wear today. Sometimes we discuss the latest movies and why it's important to make the right choices about what she sees and listens to. And we talk about friends—good ones and not-so-good ones. I encourage her to choose her friends based on what God cares about and not what's popular. This is hard for her sometimes, but at least she's beginning to understand why it's so important.

As God has allowed me to plant these spiritual seeds into Kelsey's life, I see that she's working hard to make positive changes, in spite of not receiving consistent encouragement and support from her mother.

> ### *Stay Connected Idea*
>
> *Set up a Facebook, Twitter, or Myspace account to share comments, pictures, and videos with your older grandkids. For younger ones, send cards and photos in the mail (even if they live in your town!), and encourage them to stay in touch with letters or drawings.*

Since Kelsey accepted Jesus as her personal Savior at age ten, I've made sure that she gets to church and has become a part of the youth program. Caren has never had a problem with Kelsey attending church with me, but I know if I left it up to my daughter, Kelsey would probably only see the inside of a church on Easter and Christmas.

I've witnessed Kelsey's faith grow in leaps and bounds over the past couple of years as I continue to spend time with her and plant God's seeds into her heart. I've watched in amazement as God has grown beautiful and diverse fruit from these seeds.

We both get excited when she sees her prayers get answered or she knows she made a godly choice. For example, one time I misplaced some money and asked Kelsey to help me find it. Immediately, she prayed and asked for God's guidance. It wasn't long before I heard her call from the living room. "Hey, Grandma, look what I found!" She came into the kitchen with a huge grin on her face, clutching several bills in her hand.

"Where did you find it?" I asked.

"I just prayed and asked God to help me. I started looking around and saw your Bible on the table. For some reason I felt I was supposed to open it, and when I did, there was the money!"

Not only is Kelsey growing herself, she's helping others get closer to God as well. This past summer she taught at our church's Vacation Bible School, which her younger sister, Molly, was attending. God blessed Kelsey and Molly by allowing Kelsey to play a significant role in leading Molly to accept Jesus into her heart. After the sisters prayed together, Kelsey took Molly to meet with the church's pastor and confirm her newfound faith. Since then, Kelsey has been instrumental in helping Molly learn about Jesus and grow in her faith.

Thinking about how far my granddaughter has come caused my anger over the current situation to turn to sadness, realizing how much Caren has missed out on. The Lord gently reminded me, however, to turn my concern for Kelsey and Caren over to Him one more time. Deep down I knew by doing so He would continue to guide me and help me be a strong witness of His love and power.

At that moment, I so badly wanted to hold Kelsey and remind her how much both God and I love her. Instead, I felt silenced by the Lord. I've come to understand that part of relinquishing control to the One who's in control means remembering that He is my Director and, in His grace, has given me a special role to play within my daughter's and granddaughter's lives. I must remain focused on the specific instructions this divine Director has for me.

My only job is to finish my performance well so one day I will hear Him say to me, "Well done, good and faithful servant!" (Matthew 25:21). As I play my role to the best of my ability, I trust Him to weave together a very happy ending.

Grandparents in the Bible

Isaac and Rebekah: Grandparents of Jacob

Isaac was probably at least a young adult when God tested his father, Abraham, by asking him to sacrifice Isaac as an offering. Therefore, Isaac could have resisted and overpowered elderly Abraham. However, Isaac showed incredible faith and obedience by carrying the wood for the sacrifice and willingly laying his own life down on it (Genesis 22:6–9). Surely Isaac, along with Rebekah, passed on that faith to their sons, Esau and Jacob. As Jacob became the father of the twelve tribes of Israel, Isaac and Rebekah became their grandparents, and the legacy of faith in God and the promises God had made continued.

God has provided a legacy of faith through you that will continue through your children, on to your grandchildren, and even beyond—all because of your faithfulness, obedience, and prayers.

Points to Ponder

> ➤ This grandmother's greatest obstacle was her daughter's alcohol addiction. What ungodly—and perhaps risky—behavior in your child's life presents a challenge to you? What are your options in dealing with this behavior?

> ➤ What are the practical steps this grandmother took to stay close to Kelsey? What are some practical steps you can take to be physically and emotionally close to your grandkids?

> ➤ How has going out of her way to stay close to Kelsey allowed God to open doors for Grandma to plant spiritual seeds? What opportunities are you giving God to open doors in your situation?

> ➤ What fruit have you seen in your grandchildren as a result of seeds you've planted?

> ➤ What are some specific roles that God, your Director, has given you as a grandparent?

Steps to Take

1. Ask your grandchildren what they'd most enjoy doing when you're together. Work with them and their parents to plan special grandparent/grandchild outings and activities. Pray for your time together that God would open doors for you to share spiritual truths with them.

2. The grandmother in this story learned how to send text messages in order to stay in touch with Kelsey. Choose one thing you can implement that may force you out of your comfort zone (like learning new technology or learning more about your grandkids' culture) and will help you stay closer to your grandkids.

3. This grandmother had to relinquish total control to God for her daughter's healing and her granddaughter's spiritual growth. Write down those areas of grandparenting in which you have a difficult time giving full control to God. One by one, put them into His capable hands and make a commitment to Him to not take them back.

Scriptures to Study

"Well done, good and faithful servant!" (Matthew 25:21).

❖ In what areas of your role as a grandparent will you be most proud to hear these words from the Lord?

"Faith is the substance of things hoped for, the evidence of things not seen" (Hebrews 11:1, NKJV).

❖ Faith is the ability to see God at work through the eyes of your spirit, even when you don't see the evidence of His work in the physical realm. Ask God to show you how He's working in your family when you can't see the results.

"Do not throw away your confidence; it will be richly rewarded. You need to persevere so that when you have done the will of God, you will receive what he has promised" (Hebrews 10:35–36).

❖ What is God's will for you at this time concerning your children and grandchildren? In what areas do you still need to persevere so you can receive God's promises?

One Way to Pray

Father God, help me to understand more clearly my specific role as a parent of adult children and as a grandparent. Help me to walk in this role to the best of my ability, even stepping out of my comfort zone when necessary. Show me those areas where I have not given full control of my family situation to You, and enable me to do so, once and for all, by the power of Your Holy Spirit. Also, give me ideas for how I can create opportunities for You to open doors for spiritual truths to be shared with my grandchildren. How I long to one day hear from You, "Well done, good and faithful servant!" In Jesus' name. Amen.

Prayers, Notes, or Ideas

_____

_____

_____

_____

_____

_____

_____

_____

Chapter 3

Are All the Grown-Ups Thirsty?
by Lynn Leissler

"Nana, what are they doing?" asked my four-year-old granddaughter from the back row of the church where we sat together.

I put a finger to my lips, signaling Renee to speak more quietly. She pointed to a group of people standing at the front, each with hands outstretched, and reissued her question in a stage whisper. "Well, what are they doing?"

Having forgotten it was Communion Sunday, I had neglected to explain the process. I leaned close to her ear and whispered, "This is Communion Sunday, and the grown-ups are up front to take Communion. I'll explain later." It was the best I could come up with on short notice.

Like most children, "later" for Renee is defined in mere minutes, and her inquiries continued as the plate of Communion wafers passed by. "Bread," I whispered. When the server approached our row with a tray of tiny cups, I anticipated her next question and whispered, "Grape juice."

Renee's eyes rounded to saucer size, and she abandoned her whisper. "Are all the grown-ups thirsty?"

Indeed they are. For one crazy moment, I wanted to stand and announce that Renee would deliver today's sermon. Her simple question posed with childlike astonishment captured the essence of Communion.

Renee's parents, my daughter and son-in-law, were alcohol addicts and had simultaneously relapsed. They, too, were desperately thirsty, but drank from the well of destruction rather than the well of redemption. The authorities had intervened and two days before Christmas brought my granddaughter to my home where she would stay until her parents straightened out their lives.

After church, we dashed through last-minute preparations for our Christmas celebration five hours away. Renee was excited, but after three hours on the road, her excitement gave way to anxiety. "Please, Nana, I wanna go home." Renee sobbed and whimpered with each mile that pulled her farther from her mother. She didn't understand that even if we went back, she still wouldn't be able to see her mother.

I knew the love of her aunts, uncles, and cousins, along with the treasured chaos of a family Christmas would provide much-

> ## *Ways to Combat Insecurity*
>
> *For younger grandchildren, give them a special stuffed animal, doll, or toy that will help them think of you when they're feeling insecure. Let them know that it'll be there to comfort them when you can't.*
>
> *For older kids, be sure they have your phone number in their phones and encourage them to call you anytime they need to talk. Also, teach them to express their feelings creatively, through writing, journaling, drawing, or music. As they do, they'll discover the power that such creativity has to promote comfort and security in their lives.*

needed healing. As I drove I sang Christmas carols, cooed my love, and prayed as the miles ticked away. It was a long trip.

Once we arrived at my son's home, she rallied. She thrilled at feeding his chickens and begged her uncle to build a fire in the fireplace. When the family arrived, we exchanged gifts, ate, watched an impromptu play staged by the cousins, and ate some more. Renee joined in without reservation. Two days later, she proved the bravest child, though the youngest, as we snow tubed down a nearby mountain.

Once back home, we settled into our daily routine. We continued with what had been established early on in Renee's life. When she was an infant, I often rocked her to sleep while singing hymns. Soon we added prayer and Bible stories. I had laid a foundation the best I could, considering her parents' off-kilter lives. But it was obvious that Renee associated God with her nana.

Still, sadness lay just close to the surface, and her wounds were raw. At times, she grew quiet and her features crumbled. She cried quietly, drawing from a reserve of deep pain. I held her close, and she burrowed into my arms as if she might crawl inside me and hide. As she cried, I soothed her with gentle words and whispered prayers. She was secure in my love.

Renee occasionally told stories about life at home. How could my daughter do this to her child? But I knew addiction wasn't fussy about its victims. I told Renee her mother was sick from doing the bad things Renee had witnessed.

By this time, my daughter had checked herself into a rehabilitation program, and I let Renee know her mommy was in a safe place where she could get better. Every time Renee talked to her mother on the phone, she dissolved in to a sobbing mess of longing and sorrow. I continued to rock and soothe her, and we prayed for her mother. "I want to see Mommy," Renee would plead with me. She was not allowed to visit, and I soon stopped the telephone calls. Both my daughter's sobriety and my granddaughter's emotions were too fragile.

Renee told me she needed to check on her mother, and I realized that she had already taken on the twisted role reversal of parenting my daughter. I left my frustration and anger unspoken.

I did my best to fill our time with daily routine as well as special outings. We visited the local fire department, and the fire chief lifted her into the driver's seat of the ladder truck. Everywhere we went she asked a myriad of questions, and I breathed thank-you prayers for kind folks who offered patient answers. She tagged along with me to various adult events and quickly became a pampered princess. Subconsciously, she experienced adults enjoying themselves without abusing substances.

At the end of each day, she snuggled with her stuffed animals as we read Bible stories and prayed for her family. She trusted me and felt safe enough in my home to sleep peacefully each night.

Over time, she began to initiate prayer or ask me to pray for her mom or dad. One day when it was her turn to say grace, she said in a voice of solid assurance, "Jesus … Sir … Amen." A pause punctuated each plea like an exclamation point. Then she picked up her fork and began eating. I smiled at her theology—Jesus is Lord, period. I'm guessing God smiled, too.

Part of our routine included weekly church services. On Sundays, she joined other children at Sunday school to learn about God and Jesus. On Wednesday evenings after a shared meal at church, we each attended a Bible class. Afterward she sat in a pew during choir practice and waited patiently for me. Occasionally I heard her angelic voice trilling along with us. At other times, she waved her arms in flamboyant imitation of the director. She liked church enough to ask several times a week if we would be going that day.

Sharing my home with a four-year-old presented more than a few challenges. My energy level was stretched, to say the least, yet God granted me strength for each day. It had been years since I had parented small children, so I often prayed for wisdom to know how to best parent Renee. I implemented methods that had worked with my own children, but in areas where I had failed I tried to do a better job this time around. Through it all, the Lord granted me a surprising store of patience.

I was acutely aware that each moment counted. I worried there would not be time to tell her enough about Jesus. I wanted this season to be as perfect and meaningful as possible. Did she comprehend God's love? Did she understand that prayer wasn't just something you did at Nana's house? Had she really begun to seek Him on her own?

One afternoon she put my doubts to rest. Renee played nearby while I prepared dinner, each lost in our own thoughts. Then something about her toy frustrated her, and in her impatience she muttered, "Jesus." She uttered my Lord's name in the same irreverent tone she heard at home.

With a calm voice, I said, "Renee, at Nana's house we don't use Jesus' name unless we're praying." I expected a "but-Mommy-does-it" defense.

Instead, without hesitation, she looked into my eyes and said, "Then let's pray." She set down the toy, folded her hands, and closed her eyes.

Humbled, I laid aside my stirring spoon and prayed. I thanked God that Renee and I could be together, and I prayed for her parents. After my "Amen," Renee picked up her toy, which now offered no resistance, and continued playing. I realized then that the seeds I had sown were taking root.

Another evening I prayed for her cousins, the children related by blood and marriage. My "Amen" did not sit well with Renee. She shot a scolding look my way and said, "You forgot to pray for Josh." Her uncle, a single dad, was dating a woman with a little boy. I quickly prayed mighty blessing on that little boy. A lesson learned—if you show up at your uncle's house for Christmas, you qualify as family!

Too soon, my fears were realized. Renee would be returned to her mother in a mother/child rehabilitation program. I couldn't help but cry as I told Renee the news. She asked me to stop. By sheer force of will, I did; she needed me to be strong for both of us. It thrilled me to witness her courage, but it broke my heart that such courage was necessary.

I was shocked on my first visit to the rehab facility. My sweet Renee had morphed into a very unpleasant little girl. Her manners were atrocious, and on one visit, she kicked me in the shins. I scooped her up and hugged her, giving her a gentle scolding swaddled in a blanket of love.

I see her as much as possible, though I wish it could be more. We go on outings, and she asks to go to church. I want her to retain the connections she made there, and to grow in her relationship with God. We pray over pepperoni pizza and laugh over shared memories. We talk about the kind people she met, wanting her to remember there are other ways of life than what she has experienced. When we are together, she is once more my sweet little girl.

A part of me is pleased my daughter chose to seek help and that she truly wants to be a better mother. Another part of me is frightened she might not succeed.

Once more, Renee has taught me a lesson. I need to set aside my fears, trust that God is in charge, and believe that He will take care of my granddaughter.

Yes, Renee, *all* the grown-ups are thirsty, including me.

Grandparents in the Bible

Jacob: Grandfather of Perez

Not all of Jesus' earthly ancestors were filled with faith or always acted in a godly manner. Although we can see Jacob-Israel's spiritual growth, especially toward the end of his life, we can also see some negative fruit in his descendants. Jacob's son Judah's first two sons, Er and Onan, were both wicked in God's sight and therefore, died early, leaving Er's wife, Tamar, childless. Because Jacob's sons refused to follow God's remedy, Tamar disguised herself to sleep with Judah and became pregnant, giving birth to Perez (Genesis 38). Despite their dysfunction, all of these people are in the earthly bloodline of Jesus Christ, the Lion of the tribe of Judah.

God keeps His plan on track and His promises fulfilled despite the actions of humans or the situations we find ourselves in.

Points to Ponder

> ➢ Nana knew that a daily routine would be important to Renee's healing. How did she help establish routine in Renee's life? How might establishing or reinforcing routine help your grandchild, and what specific steps can you take to generate a routine?

> ➢ How did Nana provide Renee with the security she so desperately needed? In what areas does your grandchild experience insecurity? How can you help provide this necessary security?

> ➢ What were some of the challenges Nana faced when she took Renee in? How did God help her overcome these challenges? What are some challenges that you need God to help you overcome concerning your grandchild?

> ➢ How did Nana's reaction to the way Renee treated her at the rehab facility ultimately result in securing their relationship? How might you have responded in the same situation?

> ➢ What lessons did Renee help Nana learn? How is God working through your grandchild to teach you some lessons in faith?

Steps to Take

1. If one or both of your grandchild's parents are engaged in an addictive or other dangerous behavior, it may be up to you to make the tough choices about getting help for the parents or even removing your grandchild from their care.

    Carefully and prayerfully evaluate the situation, and don't hesitate to bring in professional help—for you as well as your family. At the very least, do all you can to become more engaged in your grandchild's life.

2. If your grandchild is in a chaotic or stressful home environment, think of ways you can add routine and security to his life. Gradually incorporate these elements as you spend time together.

3. Write down the specific challenges you currently face in your relationship with your child or your grandchild. Take time to pray regularly over your list, asking for God's intervention and wisdom. As He gives you ideas for overcoming these challenges, write down what He tells you and put it into action!

Scriptures to Study

"Save me, O God, for the waters have come up to my neck. I sink in the miry depths, where there is no foothold. I have come into the deep waters; the floods engulf me" (Psalm 69:1–2).

❖ If your child is an addict or involved in another type of dangerous behavior, this psalm perfectly describes his situation. You may feel as though there is no way out for your child, and therefore, your grandchild. But don't give up! Through your prayers, love, and encouragement, God will set them free. And then you will say, along with the psalmist, "The LORD hears the needy and does not despise his captive people" (v. 33).

"The name of the LORD is a strong tower; the righteous run to it and are safe" (Proverbs 18:10).

❖ It's great that your grandchild knows she can always go to Nana for safety and security. But more importantly, you want her to see God as her ultimate security provider. How can you teach your grandchild to call on the Lord when she's feeling insecure?

"Do not grieve, for the joy of the LORD is your strength" (Nehemiah 8:10).

❖ It takes a lot of strength—supernatural strength—to
persevere through trials, to overcome family challenges, and
to keep up with young grandkids! Nehemiah 8:10 tells us we
will have this strength as we keep the joy that comes from
knowing God in our lives. How can you better keep your
heart filled with joy when you're going through difficult
times?

One Way to Pray

Jesus, I ask for Your wisdom as my family goes through challenging times. Help me to do all I can to be there for my child and my grandchild. Show me ways that I can provide necessary security and comfort to my grandchild during times of loneliness or fear. Enable me to continually walk in Your patience and unconditional love toward my family, and teach me how to stay full of Your joy so I can persevere through the trials I face. In Jesus' name. Amen.

Prayers, Notes, or Ideas

_____

_____

_____

_____

_____

_____

_____

_____

_____

_____

Chapter 4

An Unexpected Seed
by Lea Dory*

"Grandma, Grandma, Grandma," Amy repeated, flying into my arms. This welcoming salutation had become the standard greeting between my four-year-old granddaughter and me. Her response to spotting me never altered whether one day or one month had passed since our last time together. At that moment, my every concern melted into pure joy. With each inch that Amy grew, the preciousness of this gift from God exponentially increased.

Amy was baptized in my church where I have served as treasurer, elder, and participated on several committees. The baptism sacrament brought me comfort, peace, and optimism wrapped in the expectation that this baby would be raised in the Christian faith. But as the years slid by, anxiety mounted within me and I fretted about her obvious absence of spiritual training. I teetered along that fine line between sharing some of my learned wisdom with my daughter and blatantly telling her how to raise her child.

My parenting model was to give my children the freedom to find their true selves by discovering who God intended for them to become, not what I had envisioned for them to become. I wanted their beliefs to be based on their own foundation, not on mine. I had ensured that they knew all about Christianity—what it was and what it was not. But I also freed them to decide what denomination or faith group and style of worship met their needs and convictions. I wanted no less for my granddaughter.

As Amy advanced from babbling baby, to toddler, to preschooler, sadness tore a hole in my heart. Her on-the-go, career parents did not attend church, bring God into their home, or foster an understanding or appreciation for Christianity. I was tempted to ask, "Don't you think you should make time to go to church?" But I had learned during my daughter's teenage years that her skill at dodging a guilt trip was superior to mine of casting one. Other than prayer, I had no recourse.

God, however, had a plan. The summer when Amy turned five my church desperately needed a director for Vacation Bible School. The lyrics, "Here I am Lord," ricocheted in my mind, repeating themselves like an annoying chant. I tried ignoring it, but an inner voice questioned: *If I didn't do it, who would?* Without further debate, I cleared my calendar and answered the call that had seemingly come out of nowhere.

"I'm helping with VBS this year. In fact, I'm taking the lead," I confessed to my daughter. When she asked why, I wasn't quite sure how to answer, mostly because I didn't have an answer. "I don't know what I was thinking," I admitted. "It will be an incredible amount of work."

"You'll figure it out," she said. I bristled at her trite and patronizing response.

Words tumbled out before I could retrieve them, "Would you want to send Amy? It really is a fun program." Wow. Where had that come from? I never intended to just come out and ask. I prepared myself for a cool and indifferent reply. My daughter was an independent thinker, one who formed her own opinions and never hesitated to oppose me.

"That would be fine," she said. "Amy will enjoy spending the week with you."

Not exactly the response I had expected, but I gladly received it. Before my daughter could change her mind, I blurted out a quick, "Great!" and left it at that.

Preparation for VBS took center stage over the next couple of weeks, leaving no time for me to conjure up a hidden agenda for Amy's involvement. Each day of VBS week followed the same pattern: Amy and I arrived early at church with her following me around while I attended to necessary preparations. Once the day's activities began, she was off with her group. I did my thing; she did

---

Christian Event and Activity Ideas for Kids

• *Bible Study Fellowship International (**www.bsfinternational.org**): International organization that holds weekly Bible studies for adults with separate, concurrent children's lessons and activities*

• *MOPS (**www.mops.org**): International organization with regularly scheduled fellowship meetings to encourage mothers of preschoolers. Preschoolers are supervised and entertained with Bible stories, crafts, and games while the adults meet.*

• *Backyard Bible Club: Like a VBS, but held in a neighborhood backyard! Curriculum is designed for grades K-6.*

• *Christian summer camps: Age ranges generally from 5-17.*

• *Children's church choir, drama, or dance groups.*

---

hers. On the drive home, she jabbered about her VBS friends, summarized Bible stories, and contemplated how scared she was of King Pharaoh.

We filled our afternoons with throwing water balloons at Grandpa, building forts, and making use of every puzzle, book, and toy we could find. When it came time to read a story before bedtime, she marveled how God is everywhere. "Yes, and He also lives in your heart," I added. "He's always with you and will never leave you."

Amy and I both enjoyed our VBS experience. She became attached to the buzz phrase, "Fear not," repeating it often. She'd break into spontaneous monologues regarding the new things she learned about God: "He's in the clouds … He's the most powerful person in the world … We're His children …" and on and on. Her recitations reflected her attention to the daily lessons. Her newfound knowledge triggered abundant thank-you prayers from my grateful heart.

A few weeks later, I was at my daughter's babysitting Amy. Her friend Holly came to play, but after Holly's mother left, Holly cried to have her back. Without hesitation, Amy scooted close to Holly, warmly wrapped her arm around her, and whispered, "Fear not. The Lord is with you." After a quick smile from Holly, they both ran off to play.

That fall, while at my daughter's house, I mentioned my plans for visiting my childhood church. Amy overheard and begged, "I want to go too. Grandma, can I go with you?"

My daughter granted permission, and the following Sunday Amy and I attend this tiny, historic, small-town church. She sat in the pew and leafed through the hymnal, carefully examining every page, as if she were a scholar studying for a test. She didn't make a peep, and by the end of service had stolen the hearts of many in the congregation.

On the way home she asked, "Can we do that again sometime, Grandma?" What sweet music to my ears. Since that day, Amy and I have gone to church together as often as possible.

In her now six-year-old wisdom, Amy readily shares her own viewpoint about Jesus. Having yet to witness the muck of an imperfect world, she readily accepts Bible stories as truths seen through the eyes of an innocent child. The in-depth probing questions about God still lie somewhere in her future.

Through VBS God planted a seed whose growth has been gradual, one step at a time. Amy learned, believed, and shared the Good News. With a few words of expression, such as "Fear not" and "God is everywhere," along with evangelical acts of reassurance, Amy's spiritual journey had begun. Psalm 127:3 states that a child is a gift from God—a gift that keeps on giving. As Amy gave out what God had given her, others' lives were touched. Not only did Amy's parents start attending church, but Holly's did as well.

I've always asked God to protect Amy, to guide her along the path of life, and to help her mature into a joyous person filled with contentment and purpose—a person who will walk in His truths and, in one way or another, further His kingdom. I've prayed for my granddaughter every day without fail, trusting in the Lord's timing to move in her life. Now, I praise Him for using me as an instrument to bring Amy into His fold, for presenting an opportunity, a small crack in a door, which led to the opening of several other doors for now, but perhaps many more in the future.

Grandparents in the Bible

Judah: Grandfather of Hezron

"These were the sons of [Jacob-] Israel: Reuben, Simeon, Levi, Judah, Issachar, Zebulun, Dan, Joseph, Benjamin, Naphtali, Gad and Asher ...Tamar, Judah's daughter-in-law, bore him Perez and Zerah ... The sons of Perez: Hezron and Hamul" (1 Chronicles 2:1, 4–5).

God is continuing the bloodline from Abraham through King David to Jesus Christ, and He is continuing the spiritual bloodline of faith through you to your descendants.

Points to Ponder

➤ God reached this grandmother's grandchild, daughter, and a friend because of her simple obedience to help with Vacation Bible School. Is there anything that God has been asking you to do that could result in far-reaching fruit? What's holding you back from being obedient to His request?

➤ In what ways did God work through Amy's mother (without her mother even knowing it!) to help bring His plans to pass? In what areas can you trust God to work through your child to reach your grandchildren?

➤ Aside from taking Amy to VBS, in what other ways did Grandma plant spiritual seeds into her granddaughter's heart? Which of her ideas could you use in your own situation?

➤ Not all children are as evangelistic as Amy, yet God will often use kids to reach their parents. If your grandchild has a relationship with Jesus but your child does not, how can you nurture and encourage an evangelical spirit in your grandchild that will help her share Jesus with her parents?

➤ Grandma mentioned that she prays for her granddaughter daily and trusts in God's timing. Have you found it difficult to persevere in prayer for your grandchildren while you're waiting on God? If so, how can you encourage yourself to remain faithful in prayer? If not, how can you safeguard against growing weary in prayer?

Steps to Take

1. Write down anything—big or small—that God has put on your heart to do that you haven't yet done. One by one, pray over each item on your list, asking Him to help you obey His prompting in this area.

Although we can't always see it at the time, our small steps of obedience—even if they're unrelated to our prayers—may open just the right door for God to answer our prayers.

2. If you've been unable to take your grandchild to church, search out alternative Christian events or activities your grandchild may enjoy. Pray first, then take a risk by asking your child to allow your grandchild to attend. God can use any opportunity you give Him to reach a heart!

3. Develop a plan that will help you remain faithful in praying for your grandchild as well as being patient in trusting in God's timing. Your plan may include rallying a prayer partner for support and accountability, or preparing scriptures of God's faithfulness to cling to when you grow spiritually weary.

Scriptures to Study

"Does the LORD delight in burnt offerings and sacrifices as much as in obeying the voice of the LORD? To obey is better than sacrifice, and to heed is better than the fat of rams" (1 Samuel 15:22).

❖ Sometimes it's easier for us to make great sacrifices for the Lord instead of obeying what He's told us to do. Yet God requires our obedience over sacrifice. Determine if there are areas where you've sacrificed instead of obeyed. Take a moment to ask for the Lord's forgiveness and for His help in obeying Him now and in the future.

"Your love, O LORD, reaches to the heavens, your faithfulness to the skies" (Psalm 36:5).

❖ We never know who or what God may use to bring an answer to our prayers. But we do know that when we pray according to His Word He is always faithful to answer. Don't try to figure out how He's going to do it, just trust that He will!

"… Imitate those who through faith and patience inherit what has been promised" (Hebrews 6:12).

❖ Which is most difficult for you: having faith that your prayers will be answered, or being patient while you wait for answers to your prayers? How can you strengthen these two areas so you can inherit God's promises for your family?

One Way to Pray

Lord, I know that You can use any situation or opportunity to draw my family to You. Help me to be open to anything You may want to use and not unknowingly close a door of opportunity due to disobedience or not discerning Your voice. Strengthen me by the power of Your Holy Spirit as I endeavor to persevere in prayer for my family. Encourage me through Your Word and through others to never give up and to patiently wait for Your perfect timing. In Jesus' name. Amen.

Prayers, Notes, or Ideas

_____

_____

_____

_____

_____

_____

_____

_____

_____

_____

Chapter 5

Just Keep Prayin'
by Abigail Paul*

Grandma's lips moved as she scooped hot homemade rolls from the cooking sheet with her bare hands. Her lips kept moving as she stacked still-sizzling golden-brown fried chicken onto the platter. As a young girl, I was enthralled watching Grandma's lips continue their quiet, constant motion while she stirred flour gravy in her black cast-iron skillet and finished the evening meal preparations.

"Who are you talking to?" I asked from my perch on the old wooden kitchen stool my grandpa had made.

She chuckled, wiping her hands on her well-stained apron. Her subtle nervous laugh revealed her embarrassment that I had caught her. "Oh, I guess I was just prayin'," she said.

It wouldn't be the last time I watched my grandmother's lips moving as she went about daily tasks. It was a regular occurrence. I could tell when things bothered Grandma, though she never said much to me about her worries. Instead, she consistently took them to Jesus, probably never realizing how much I was watching and learning.

My family went to the same church as Grandma and Grandpa. Each week after church, we'd gather for lunch at my grandparents' house. I looked forward to these special meals, knowing I could count on all sorts of delicious foods, including homemade apple and lemon pies—in addition to Grandpa's wonderful stories while we ate. I loved going to Grandma's and Grandpa's. It had become my safe place in my otherwise anxious young life.

My parents began to argue often, especially on the weekends, and most especially on the drive to my grandparents after church. I made it a point to ride home with Grandma under the pretense of helping her prepare our meal. I did enjoy being with my grandparents and doing the tasks Grandma gave me, but I had ulterior motives—escaping the gut-wrenching fights and constant tension in my parents' car. Riding in Grandpa's old but pristine, blue-green pick-up became a weekly ritual.

An Encouraging Word

"Preach the Gospel at all times and when necessary use words."
(St. Francis of Assisi)

"Prayer is the natural and joyous breathing of the spiritual life by which the heavenly atmosphere is inhaled and then exhaled in prayer."
(Andrew Murray)

One day after church I sat between my grandparents in that old pick-up, bouncing all the way down the country road that led to their house. I stared out the window at the green rolling hills. I can still see the view all these years later, even though I wasn't thinking about the view at the time. I doubt I even noticed how beautiful it really was. Instead, I was grieving my parents' failing marriage. "Why do Mom and Dad fight so much?" I asked Grandma. "I keep praying and praying for God to help them. Why don't things between them ever change?"

"I don't know, honey," Grandma replied. She took my hand and held it tightly between both of hers. "We just have to keep praying."

And we did.

Things never did change for my parents. When I see the Lord face-to-face, I'd like to ask Him why some prayers don't seem to get the results we pray for. I suspect it has something to do with the stubbornness of human will and God allowing us to make our own choices. But even though my parents kept fighting, I knew the Lord was there for me, and there *were* results to all those prayers—my growing faith and dependence on Him.

As a little girl, I hid in the bathroom with my Bible and Raggedy Ann doll when the fighting escalated. Later, in my middle-school years, I started journaling and filled pages with all kinds of prayers and the deepest thoughts of my heart. Sometimes all I could do was scribble large, jutting circles and lines in random, angry patterns, but through it all, I followed my grandmother's admonition and kept prayin'.

Because of my grandmother's example, I learned what it was like to depend on God, even when life brought pain and disappointment—or maybe, especially when life brought pain and disappointment. I learned how to turn to Him when the angry voices rose to ear-piercing levels or when the shattering of a broken dish thrown across the kitchen by my mother echoed up the stairwell. I clung to Him during the early mornings when I heard the car's tires screech out of the driveway, making me wonder if my mom was coming back. I sang "Faith-Walkin' People" as I prayed and grieved when my mom did leave us for an extended period, not telling us where she went, only leaving a note on my Toyota saying she loved me and would be in touch.

Throughout all those years, God continued to meet my need for emotional security in the quiet, loving acceptance of my grandparents' home. I often spent the night with them, resting from my continual inner turmoil. Grandma taught me a lot of things—like how to sew a seam and make to-die-for piecrusts. Not once did she criticize my mom or dad. She only kept loving, cooking, sewing, and praying—mostly praying; her lips in constant motion even when no sounds came out. And I kept watching, and developing in my faith.

My parents finally divorced the year after I graduated from college. I married and had children of my own. Life soon turned chaotic with four children aged six and younger. Financial struggles became the norm as we endeavored to live on one salary so I could stay home with the little ones. But no matter what I faced, Grandma's teaching and example stayed close to my heart. The kids and I learned to pray through our chaotic preschool days. We prayed when we snacked or napped or had a special need. Bedtime was prayer time. When I struggled with temper or the kids bickered, it meant it was time to pray. Looking back, I was simply mirroring what Grandma had taught me: Prayer was not meant to be relegated to quiet, alone times with God or church services; it was an on-going, day-by-day, minute-by-minute experience.

One week in particular pulled at me from every direction. My husband was unemployed, I learned that someone close to me had an illness said to be incurable, my father-in-law had a heart attack from which we were told he may not recover, and my sister-in-law had a difficult week-long labor, causing us to fear for her and the baby. In the middle of it all, a card arrived in the mail. Inside the card was a bookmark on which was written my name and the words: "Little one, dependent on God."

As I prayed and journaled about the experience, I sensed the Lord whisper, "You've always been My little one. Even as a child when you felt like the adult in your out-of-control home, I was teaching you to crawl up on My lap and depend on Me." The Lord's words solidified my identity as God's little one, totally dependent on Him. This security carried me through that hard week and the following months that included the death of my beloved father-in-law and a long season of unemployment for my husband.

Today I'm the mother of four teenagers. Our family has weathered the near-death of my husband; various learning disabilities, unexpected illnesses, and surgeries in the children; and financial upheaval. With each trial stretching my faith a little further, I've grown closer to God. Dependence on my Lord and the comfort and strength that develops during times of prayer are most precious to me. I cling to God as Grandma taught me to, knowing He is my strength and my song, just as He was for her.

Grandma's been gone several years now, but her legacy lives on. For her eightieth birthday, my brother and I wrote a song about her. I can only hope that someday my own children and grandchildren could sing these words about me—and see my lips move in prayer and praise to Him continually throughout the day.

Just prayin' throughout her day,
She is always with you.
Just prayin' throughout her day,
That is Grandma's way.

Grandparents in the Bible

Perez: Grandfather of Ram

"The sons of Perez: Hezron and Hamul … The sons born to Hezron were: Jerahmeel, Ram and Caleb" (1 Chronicles 2:5, 9).

God included many people in the bloodline of Christ who we may not know much about, yet their names are recorded in God's eternal Word. You may feel insignificant and unknown, but you are known to God. Not only is your name recorded in His Book of Life, but He is using you to ensure that your descendants names are also written in His Book of Life.

Points to Ponder

➢ Do you sometimes feel like the young granddaughter in this story when she kept "praying and praying" but nothing ever changed in her parents' relationship? What do you do when it seems as if your prayers go unanswered? What was the grandmother's response to her granddaughter's frustration with this problem? Do you agree with her response? Why or why not?

➢ How did Grandma's example of prayer affect her granddaughter, even years later, when she had children of her own? What things are you passing on to your grandchild that have such staying power?

➢ What was the main lesson the author learned about prayer through her grandmother? How can you teach this same lesson to your grandchild?

➢ It's often said that trials will either make us bitter or better. Did the granddaughter grow bitter or better through her trials? Why? What safeguards do you have in place to ensure that you grow better and closer to God through your trials?

➢ This grandma left her grandkids a legacy of prayer simply by living out her faith in front of them. In what ways are you living out your faith in front of your grandchild? What legacy would you most like to be known for leaving your family?

Steps to Take

1. Take time to say heart-felt prayers with your grandchild. Pray before meals, before bed, before you start your day, before you travel (even to the grocery store!), and anytime you need help or direction. Encourage your grandchild to pray too, and begin to instill in her the habit of ongoing prayer throughout the day.

2. One thing the author remembered about her grandmother is that "not once did she criticize my mom or dad." Criticism can be quite tempting, especially if your child has disappointed you by turning from God. Ask for forgiveness for any critical words you have spoken over your child then ask the Holy Spirit to help you to only speak positive words of blessing concerning your child. Your grandchild will surely notice!

3. Prayerfully consider the spiritual legacy you want to leave your grandchild. Write it out as a mission statement, and place it where you'll see it often. Be purposeful in doing all you can to fulfill your mission of bringing this legacy to pass.

Scriptures to Study

"Be joyful always; pray continually; give thanks in all circumstances, for this is God's will for you in Christ Jesus" (1 Thessalonians 5:16–18).

- ❖ At first thought, Paul's command to "pray continually" seems nearly impossible. But when you approach prayer like this grandmother did and view it simply as carrying on a conversation with the Lord, you'll find that it's not only possible but necessary to help you through your day.

  Do you have difficulty having an ongoing conversation with God? If you struggle in this area, ask God to help you learn to talk to Him during the day just as you would a good friend. Begin the practice of talking to God then listening on and off throughout your day. The more you do it, the more you'll want to do it!

"You are the light of the world. A city on a hill cannot be hidden. Neither do people light a lamp and put it under a bowl. Instead they put it on its stand, and it gives light to everyone in the house. In the same way, let your light shine before men, that they may see your good deeds and praise your Father in heaven" (Matthew 5:14–16).

❖ When we are filled with the light of the Holy Spirit, we don't have to work to produce it in our lives—it just naturally flows out of us, just like it did with this grandmother. Think of those in your life who shined their light before you. Chances are, they didn't even realize what they were doing at the time or how they've affected you. Just stay full of God, and allow His light in you to shine from every part of your being. You'll impact your grandchild more than you'll ever realize.

"Whatever you have learned or received or heard from me, or seen in me—put it into practice. And the God of peace will be with you" (Philippians 4:9).

❖ Here, Paul was encouraging the church at Philippi to learn from his example of what it means to be a disciple and do it themselves. This is exactly what the author did in this story. She learned from her grandmother how to pray, and when she went through her own hard times, she put those lessons into practice. The result was God's peace despite her circumstances.

What can you pass onto your grandchild that will bring about God's peace when he puts it into practice?

One Way to Pray

Thank You, Father God, for the privilege of being able to pass along a spiritual legacy to my grandchild. Help me to be intentional as to what this legacy will be and to be mindful of my actions and words that will affect the legacy I leave. I pray that You will enable me to live out a positive example of Your love, forgiveness, and hope in front of my grandchild at all times. Help me, Lord, as I endeavor to stay in a place of continual fellowship with You throughout my day so my heart will overflow with the fruit of the Spirit when I'm with my grandchild. In Jesus' name. Amen.

Prayers, Notes, or Ideas

_____

_____

_____

_____

_____

_____

_____

_____

_____

PART 2

The Challenge of
Long-Distance Relationships

When you dreamed of grandparenting, you didn't have in mind doing it long distance. But your child moved far away. Maybe he went to college and found a career that took him to a town away from home. Now he lives and works, and is raising his family, a long distance from you. Or maybe after your daughter married, her spouse's job moved them across the country. Or possibly you're the one who moved. You had to pull up stakes and leave the grandkids behind. You always dreamed of having your grandkids close by—able to come visit on a whim. You never imagined your child could move so far away, let alone whisk your grandkids off to cities and states and countries unknown.

Maybe you're no longer in the same city with your grandchildren. Maybe now you're not even in the same state. For some grandparents, you're not even in the same country!

You know that there is no physical distance in prayer. And you know God has promised He will go with us (or our grandchildren) wherever we or they go. Psalm 139:9 sums it up by saying, "If I settle on the far side of the sea, even there your hand will guide me, your right hand will hold me fast." And yet you long to see them. Just as the apostle John longed to see his converts, writing, "I have much to write to you, but I do not want to use paper and ink. Instead, I hope to visit you and talk with you face to face, so that our joy maybe complete" (2 John 1:12).

Oh how you long to be there. In person. But you just can't. At least not very often. You long to make a difference in their lives, to impart your faith, to watch them grow in every way, including spiritually. But you can only be there once in a while. You can only get together a few times a year, or once a year, or perhaps not even that often.

So what can you do? What do you do when you can't get together? How can you possibly influence your grandkids for Christ when you're miles or states away, or in opposite hemispheres?

And then on those rare and precious occasions when you *can* get together, when you're there with your grandkids in person— whether you've gone to them or they've come to you—how can you pack in as much God-time as possible? How do you fill the time you *do* have with them with important, spiritually relevant activities?

In the following stories you'll read about parents who are overcoming the obstacles of living hours away—or a half a world away—from their grandkids. You'll read about one grandma and grandpa who worried they couldn't keep up with their grandkids, but then God gave them a creative summer idea that was so fun, by Christmas the kids were asking when they could do it again! You'll also discover some amazing places you can go and wonderful resources available to help you pass along your faith during a meaningful vacation. You'll read how some grandmas are making use of modern technologies to stay in touch with their far-away grandchildren and at the same time are using good old-fashioned books, or creating their own stories, to impart their faith. What about when you're the one who is far off and the grandkids only rarely get to come and visit? Read how a missionary works with her grandkids when they come to one South American mission field, and how they continue their work long-distance when the grandkids return home.

You'll find dozens of ideas and resources to inspire you with ways to reach out to your grandchildren through the distance, no matter how many miles. You'll see living examples of grandparents who are making it work, who are having an influence on their long-distance grandkids. You'll be inspired to explore technologies that magically bridge the miles, schedule a life-changing vacation, or plan some very fun, very special activities for just you and your grandkids—and God, of course.

So grab your suitcase! We're headed off to faraway lands and fun adventures—all geared toward influencing your grandchildren to know the God who created, and is Lord of, the whole world!

Chapter 6

Gone Camping
by Barbara Ann Baranowski

"Nana, when's our next camp?" nine-year-old Brennan asked as we shared a good-bye hug following another year of "Nana Camp."

"Yeah, when it is?" Andrew, seven, echoed, hoping for an instant replay of Bible verse basketball before his parents came. If you ever attended camp as a child, you may still hum a camp song now and then, or find a Popsicle-stick wall hanging bearing a glittery Bible verse among your childhood treasures. I sighed, knowing that our grandchildren would have to wait a full year for the next Nana Camp.

But I was warmed by their enthusiasm. I hadn't exactly envisioned myself as camp director at age sixty-two, but my husband and I had just finished our fifth successful year. Now, sipping a cup of tea in my eerily quiet kitchen, my aching muscles recounted a week's worth of fun. I thought about the events that preceded the first summer and was reminded of how God answered a grandmother's prayer.

Our four grandchildren do not live nearby, so I had prayed that God would help my husband and me with the challenges of long-distance grandparenting—especially when it came to sharing our faith. I was eager to get started on something—but frustrated because I wasn't sure what. It wasn't long until my prayer was answered.

"I brought you back a wonderful grandparenting book from the fall ladies' conference," my friend Linda said, as she stood on my doorstep. I had read others, so I wondered what could be so attractive and different about this one. I eagerly read the book, but when I got to the chapter titled "Nana's Summer Camp," I knew I had found my answer. The idea of providing a "camp-like" experience for our out-of-town grandchildren, where we could offer activities, family experiences, and lessons from the Bible captivated me. Could I do something like that? Even more, would my husband and I have the stamina to host four young energetic campers? Over the next few months, my mind swirled with various possibilities, and soon I had a list of camping ideas. Thoughts of sharing our love for God in a memorable setting swelled our hearts and danced through our longing spirits.

During the winter and early spring, I roamed through stores searching for age-appropriate books, stickers, coloring pages, prizes, and crafts for my theme. Every purchase brought excitement as I placed it in my camp storage box. I ordered blank-paged books for the children to decorate—illustrating the theme, Bible verse, and week's activities with stickers, drawings, photos, or words. I imagined their smiling, intent expressions as they busily decorated their keepsake books (and selves) with glitter glue, paint, and markers. I'd planned for them to illustrate the Bible stories they learned or put crafts inside. I thought about the games we would play, not only allowing the children to have fun, but to get to know each other better, since our grandchildren are from two different daughters. Since they don't live close to one another, this would be the perfect time for cousin interaction.

Anticipating each annual topic to build on the previous year's theme, I decided to start simple the first year: "God Made Everything Great!" The following summers' themes would include "God Loves Me," "Jesus Is My Shepherd," "Discovering Jesus," and "Following Jesus." Just like a camp counselor, I formulated a daily schedule of activities for mornings and afternoons, leaving time for free play. Mornings included a story, Bible verse, song, crafts, and games. Afternoons were reserved for water fun, movies, or visiting the zoo.

Tips for starting your own "Nana Camp"

- *Pick a theme and choose activities that support it.*
- *If you have multiple ages, plan for the middle age of the group, and let the older children help with the lessons.*
- *Plan activities around your expertise, whether that's art, science, or baking!*
- *Create opportunities for the kids to ask Jesus into their hearts.*

My plans included honoring each camper at dinner by serving his or her favorite meal. What a perfect opportunity to get to know each grandchild better as we discussed favorite colors, sports, and friends. It would also be a great time to review the day's lesson and scripture verse. I decided to laminate the verses and put them on a cute key chain, so they could take them home and practice them. Each year more would be added.

When the time approached for the first camp experience, I sent invitations. As I addressed each one, I prayed for that grandchild, asking the Lord to water the seeds of truth that were being sown into the soil of tender hearts.

Now, recalling each summer's blessings, I am humbled at the way God has allowed my husband and me to have a part in His life-changing work. On subsequent visits to our grandchildren, we relive the memories of Nana Camp as we open the precious keepsake book. They never tire of opening the books again and again. It's a thrill to see the fruit of our labors as the kids remember the scriptures and lessons they've learned with each camp. It's obvious that they've used them to grow closer to the Lord. I've also found that throughout the year the children ask questions or make comments based on things we have discussed at camp. The truths learned at camp never seem to be far from their minds.

Not only has God blessed us through the camp, but He has also inspired others. For example, on the last day of camp, we slip into our theme-imprinted T-shirts and head out for a day of thrills at an amusement park or another tourist site. Besides helping us stay together, the shirt serves as a witness to others. Often strangers have commented, "Great idea," or "That saying is so true."

Each year as we enjoy our final camp moments together, I'll smile and remind our grandchildren, "Remember, Nana Camp can be any day—just revisit the beautiful memories stored in your keepsake book." With a full heart, I thank God for His special design for grandparents. Soon I will be lost again in plans for next year's camp, ready to hang a sign on my door that says, "Gone camping."

Grandparents in the Bible

Ram: Great-grandfather of Salmon (whose wife was Rahab)

"Ram was the father of Amminadab, and Amminadab the father of Nahshon, the leader of the people of Judah. Nahshon was the father of Salmon…" (1 Chronicles 2:10–11).

Salmon took Rahab as his wife. Our Bible text calls Rahab a prostitute, although Josephus and other sources call her an "innkeeper" (NIV Study Bible [1985] note on Joshua 2:1).

If your family is filled with scoundrels or criminals, keep in mind Jesus' earthly family history was as well, yet the names of three women, including Rahab's, are honored by being included in the genealogy of Jesus for all eternity in God's Word. God can use anyone whose heart willingly turns to Him.

Points to Ponder

➤ If you're not able to get away for a camping experience with your grandkids, what are some creative ways you could have a "Nana Camp" at home?

➤ If you were to hold a camp, what would be your theme and your main Bible verses? Who could you enlist to help you with resources, activity ideas, and preparation?

➤ This nana was very organized and thorough in her preparations—even including making plans for future camps. If this isn't your style, how might you work with your personality and interests to create a memorable experience for your grandchildren?

➤ What are some ideas for keepsakes you could have your grandchildren make when you're together that will not only remind them of being with you but also of what they learned spiritually?

➤ This grandmother sacrificed much time, effort, and energy to plan an experience that her grandchildren will remember and cherish for the rest of their lives. Honestly consider what you are willing to do to create such spiritual memories for your grandkids. What are your limits, if any?

Steps to Take

1. To prepare for a "Nana Camp" list what steps would be involved, the supplies you'll need, the lessons you want to teach, and the crafts or activities you'd like to do. Pray over each step of the process, asking for God's grace, wisdom, and provision.

2. If you'd rather not hold a "Nana Camp," ask the Lord for other ideas of how you can create memorable spiritual moments for your grandchildren. Consider what would be involved in the preparation of each idea, then choose one you can begin putting together.

3. Decide on a keepsake craft you can make with your grandkids when you're together that will help them remember spiritual principles or scripture verses. Purchase the supplies needed for the keepsake to have ready for the next time your grandkids visit.

Scriptures to Study

"These commandments that I give you today are to be upon your hearts. Impress them upon your children … Tie them as symbols on your hands and bind them on your foreheads. Write them on the doorframes of your houses and on your gates" (Deuteronomy 6:6–9).

❖ The nana in this story obeyed this scripture by not only teaching her grandchildren about God's Word but also by sending them home with scripture-reminder key chains. How are you currently keeping God's Word before your grandchildren's eyes and in their hearts? What could you do differently to make more of an impact?

"But you will receive power when the Holy Spirit comes on you; and you will be my witnesses in Jerusalem, and in all Judea and Samaria, and to the ends of the earth" (Acts 1:8).

❖ Grandma and her grandkids took their love for Jesus to the streets by wearing scripture-based T-shirts from their "Nana Camp." What are some ways that you could turn the time you have with your grandchildren into an opportunity to be a witness to others?

"Jesus said, 'Let the little children come to me, and do not hinder them, for the kingdom of heaven belongs to such as these'" (Matthew 19:14).

❖ There are many vehicles we can use to help our grandkids come to Jesus. Having a "Nana Camp" is just one. But whichever vehicle you choose, the most important thing is to create a safe and comfortable environment for your grandchildren to freely come to Jesus and not be hindered in any way.

One Way to Pray

Heavenly Father, I know You see the struggles and frustrations I face trying to grandparent from a distance. Help me to find creative and fun ways to teach my grandchildren about You and Your Word whether we're together or apart. I thank You for the precious times we do have together. I ask that You help me make the most of these times by providing opportunities to sow eternal seeds into their lives. Enable me to create memorable moments that will last them a lifetime and point them back to You. In Jesus' name. Amen.

Prayers, Notes, or Ideas

_____

_____

_____

_____

_____

_____

_____

_____

_____

_____

Chapter 7

Passing Along the Faith
by Kathie Mitchell

"This is the best motel room ever!" nine-year-old Dominic said, swaying on a hammock swing suspended from a huge concrete tree growing out of the floor. His seven-year-old brother, Gabriel, hurried over for his turn on the swing.

"There's more," my husband said, leading our two grandsons up the spiral staircase inside the concrete tree. "Check this out." The tree-top loft held a pull-down Murphy bed, a table with chairs, and a second television, all set in a jungle theme. "You boys get to sleep up here."

Dominic and Gabriel's eyes grew wide. "Cool!" they shouted in unison.

Upstairs and down, the room had been painted to resemble a tropical jungle. Toucans sat on tree branches, while tigers peeked out behind wide leaves. Imitation vines hung everywhere.

My husband and I grinned at each other. The tree house room reserved for the first night of a four-day trip to Ohio was a hit. But the main goal of our mini-vacation would take place over the next two days when we visited the Creation Museum.

We believe nothing in life is more important than knowing Christ personally and obeying His teachings. Although Dominic and Gabriel are being raised by Christian parents and are in church regularly, the boys are constantly bombarded with anti-biblical ideas through media, public education, and even friends.

Statistics show that only 9 percent of Christians have a biblical worldview, or use the principles laid out in the Bible as the basis for everyday decisions and actions. Even though we live several hours away from our grandsons, my husband and I want to lend a hand in helping the boys become part of that 9 percent.

To cultivate a biblical worldview, our grandsons need to know that the Bible is true, what it teaches, and learn how to apply those teachings to their lives—a rather daunting task in today's culture where the existence of God is often denied and the Bible dismissed as myth. After hearing about a new museum near Cincinnati, Ohio, that shows how science and archeology support the Bible—instead of oppose it—I decided to research it further online. This could be just the thing we've been looking for to help reinforce a biblical worldview in our grandkids.

"Hey, Mike," I called to my husband when I first began researching a vacation spot. "Come look at this. The museum has a state-of-the-art planetarium."

Mike peered over my shoulder and read off the computer screen. "Cosmic journey … rocket through galaxies. Impressive."

"There's also a dinosaur den, special-effects theater, and life-size exhibits that bring the Bible to life," I added. "Sounds fantastic."

Mike nodded. "Dominic and Gabriel are old enough to enjoy a museum. It would be a great place to take them sometime."

I had to agree.

After a year of saving and planning, that 'sometime' finally became a reality. On the day of our departure, we pulled out of the driveway a little after 5:00 in the morning.

"You boys can go back to sleep," Mike said. "It's going to be a long day."

"I'm too excited," Gabriel said. "Grammy, can you put in one of my Bible story CDs?"

"Or one of mine?" Dominic added.

I laughed. "We have a good ten-hour drive ahead of us. That's plenty of time to listen to them all."

For the trip, both Dominic and Gabriel brought along an inexpensive digital camera to record their adventures. As we drove across Ohio, the flat land amazed the boys. They were used to the mountains and rolling hills of Pennsylvania.

"I'm taking pictures of this to show Mom and Dad," Dominic said, aiming his camera out the window.

"Me too," Gabriel said, digging his camera out of its case.

Late in the afternoon we pulled into the motel parking lot and checked in. "We reserved a special surprise for tonight," Mike told the boys as he unlocked the door to the tree house room.

The next morning, the boys said a sad good-bye to the tree house room before we headed to the car and set out to find the Creation Museum. Before long, we were driving through the gate to the museum complex. The boys hopped out of the car, ready for adventure. And they didn't have to wait long.

"Look, there's a dinosaur!" Dominic whipped out his camera and began taking pictures of the life-size, metal sauropod standing outside the museum's entrance.

"Get a picture of me standing by it," Gabriel said. "Then I'll take one of you."

"Look at all the fish," Dominic said, pulling out his camera as we entered the waterfall exhibit.

"And turtles," Gabriel added, snapping pictures through the exhibit's glass sides.

Biblically Centered Vacations

- *Creation Museum—Petersburg, Kentucky; includes a planetarium, petting zoo, and botanical gardens; http://creationmuseum.org*
- *The Holy Land Experience—Orlando, Florida; features live shows, movies, and replicas and exhibits from first-century living; http://www.holylandexperience.com*
- *Alpha Omega Institute—Grand Junction, Colorado; holds annual Creation Vacations and Discover Creation Tours; http://www.discovercreation.org*
- *Ark Encounter—Williamsburg, Kentucky; Noah's Ark theme park; scheduled to open spring, 2014.*

The boys then scooted over to the fossil displays and began taking more pictures. "Guys, come here," Mike said, pulling Dominic and Gabriel aside. "We have two days to tour the museum, but we'll never get through it if you take a dozen pictures of every single thing you see. And even your digital cameras can run out of space."

The boys settled down and we continued on to the Dinosaur Dig where two archeologists sat on a rocky mound jutting out of the middle of the floor. Partially excavated dinosaur bones sprawled across the outcropping. The dig's campsite display took up one side of the room.

The boys hurried over to a box with "TOUCH A REAL FOSSIL" written on the side in large white letters. A bone made of stone lay inside. Dominic and Gabriel ran their fingers over the fossil.

"How are fossils made?" Dominic asked.

"Well … a simple version is this," I answered. "In a flood, dirt and stones mix with the fast-moving water. Some plants and animals get caught in the muddy mixture and are quickly buried when the water suddenly slows down and the dirt and stones sink to the bottom. Before the plant or animal has time to decay, it's turned into stone, fossilized."

"It would take a big flood to bury a dinosaur," Dominic said.

"Can you think of a big flood?" Mike asked. "Big enough to bury lots of dinosaurs?"

"Noah's flood!"

We resumed our tour through the museum, enjoying each display. The Garden of Eden exhibit filled an entire room with life-size trees, animals, lush vegetation, and Adam enjoying some animal friends.

"Where's the snake that lied to Eve?" Gabriel asked.

"Keep looking for it," Mike said as we continued along the winding garden pathway. "I'm sure it's here somewhere."

"There it is," Gabriel said, pointing up into a tree. "And Eve's holding the fruit."

Over the two days touring the Creation Museum, the grandsons watched a planetarium show, fed a camel and other animals at the petting zoo, toured the Dinosaur Den filled with life-size creatures, and walked through Bible history.

During the second day, Dominic grew quiet at one point and looked rather thoughtful. "I really don't know much about the Bible," he said, realizing for the first time that there's more to following Jesus than simply hearing familiar Bible stories over and over again in Sunday school.

His statement made quite an impression on us. A few weeks after arriving back home, we bought him a kid's daily Bible, a one-year chronological Bible written especially for children.

"How's the daily Bible reading coming?" I asked Dominic later.

"Really good. It's helping me understand everything a lot better." He paused. "Grammy, can we go to the Creation Museum again sometime?"

"Absolutely!" I answered. I then realized that all of our saving and planning for our Creation Museum vacation was well worth it, as it planted seeds in both of our grandkids to want to learn about God and His Word on a deeper level. And to me, those seeds are the greatest gift we can give our grandkids—no matter what the cost.

Grandparents in the Bible

Nahshon: Grandfather of Boaz

"Ram the father of Amminadab, Amminadab the father of Nahshon, Nahshon the father of Salmon, Salmon the father of Boaz, whose mother was Rahab ..." (Matthew 1:4–5a).

Salmon, and his wife, Rahab (the former prostitute), were the parents of Boaz, the famous Kinsman Redeemer who saved the foreigner Ruth. The instructions of God were obviously handed down to Boaz from godly grandparents and parents. Boaz took God's commandments to heart and lived them out well.

Points to Ponder

➢ In this story, the grandmother commented, "To cultivate a biblical worldview, [grandchildren] need to know that the Bible is true, what it teaches, and learn how to apply those teachings to their lives." These grandparents chose to take their grandkids to the Creation Museum to help communicate these truths and foster a biblical worldview. What vacation experiences could you share with your grandchild to help him cultivate a biblical worldview?

➢ If you're not able to take such a vacation with your grandchild, what are some fun ways you could share God's creation or other aspects of His Word in your geographic area? (e.g.: nature hikes, visits to a planetarium or natural history museum, a working farm to discuss biblical seed and harvest principles, etc.)

➢ One reason the grandparents in this story went to the Creation Museum with their grandchildren was to counter the anti-biblical messages their grandkids hear and see. Is this also a concern of yours regarding your own grandchild? How can you use your influence as a grandparent—even from a distance—to counter the messages your grandchild receives?

➤ Taking grandchildren out of state on a vacation can get expensive. How could you financially plan and budget—or maybe share expenses with another family member—for a vacation that could result in your grandchild's spiritual growth? What sacrifices (of both time and money) would you be willing to make to enable such a trip?

➤ Consider a "stay-cation" with your grandchild instead of going away. What age-appropriate resources (Internet, DVDs, games, books) could you use to help teach your grandchild biblical truths and promote a Christian worldview?

Steps to Take

1. List possible vacation options that may provide an opportunity to share God's creation or other biblical principles with your grandchild. Begin researching each option then develop a savings plan for the vacation you choose.

2. If it's more feasible than a long vacation, plan a few weekend getaways with your grandchild that could help foster a biblical worldview.

3. Consider what specific aspects of a biblical worldview or what spiritual truths you most want to impart to your grandchild. Research the various resources available on these topics that you want to share with him the next time you're together.

Scriptures to Study

Read Genesis 1.

❖ The ramifications of knowing that we have been created by a loving God and that we are not simply here by accident run deep. It's important for children to not only know about the Creation in Genesis 1, but to know how to defend it in the face of an evolutionary-biased society.

"You made [man] ruler over the works of your hands; you put everything under his feet: all flocks and herds, and the beasts of the field, the birds of the air, and the fish of the sea ..." (Psalm 8:6–8).

❖ Not only did God make the whole world, He made it for us! He made people—His most-prized creation—to rule over all the other works of His hands. This truth counters today's secular mindset of worshipping creation instead of the Creator. How can you instill in your grandchild the important balance of being good stewards of the world God gave us yet keeping its role in perspective?

"For since the creation of the world God's invisible qualities— his eternal power and divine nature—have been clearly seen, being understood from what has been made, so that men are without excuse" (Romans 1:20).

❖ Everything in nature—from the tiniest ant to the largest galaxy—screams that there is a God. How can you help your grandchild learn to see the power and majesty of his Creator all around him?

One Way to Pray

Wonderful Lord, show me a fun place where I can take my grandchild to help her learn about You and reinforce the biblical principles I'm teaching her. If it's best for us to take a short weekend trip or even stay close to home, I ask that You would show me that as well, and give me creative ideas of where we could go together. I also ask for Your provision of both time and money to help create an experience for her that she will remember for years to come. Protect her, Lord, from the secularism that surrounds her. Give her a heart to always follow Your Word and build her life on a solid biblical foundation. In Jesus' name. Amen.

Prayers, Notes, or Ideas

Chapter 8

Liking Skyping
by Rev. Annalee Davis

Just before his seminary graduation, my son Larry called to tell me he was applying for a senior pastor position in a church.

"That's wonderful! Where is it?" I asked, hoping to hear him respond "in New Jersey." I silently prayed a quick prayer: *Please, Lord, anywhere closer than Massachusetts!*

"It's in Maine."

Sudden silence filled our conversation.

"It's a great church, and they need a pastor right away," Larry continued. "We'll move in June if I'm asked to serve."

"Maine?"

"Yes, Mom. Maine." I could tell by Larry's tone he knew I was not pleased.

"That's further than we are from each other now! How long will it take to drive there?"

"I don't know. Eight hours?"

My heart sank. My granddaughters would be even further away from me. *When will I see them? What about the holidays? Lord, that's not what I prayed for!*

I took a deep breath and assured my son, "If that's where the Lord wants you, then that's where you'll need to go. I'll support you wherever the Lord leads."

I knew it wouldn't be easy having an adult child involved in ministry. Memories of packing up our family while living in New Jersey and heading for pastoral ministry in Michigan were still easy to recall. My sons had been only two and four years old then—and I was taking my mother's only grandchildren 700 miles away from her loving arms. It broke both her heart and mine.

Back then, letters and phone calls were the only means of communication. Expensive long-distance charges kept our conversations short. We saw each other only twice a year during vacations. My parents missed so much of their grandsons' growing years. I didn't want that to happen to me.

An Encouraging Word

"The best babysitters, of course, are the baby's grandparents. You feel completely comfortable entrusting your baby to them for long periods, which is why most grandparents flee to Florida." (Dave Barry)

My son prepared for his call by going to Messiah College in Pennsylvania. After graduating and getting married, Larry and his wife moved near the campus. That's where my first grandchild was born. In September 2000, I traveled to see this precious baby girl. As Larry placed Adrienne in my arms, I rejoiced that I was alive and well enough to hold my firstborn's first child. The joy of holding her was immeasurable.

I lovingly wrapped my arms around Adrienne and held her close to my heart. I gently placed my cheek next to her velvet skin and whispered, "I'm Grandma, and I love you."

Not long after Adrienne's birth, my son and daughter-in-law moved to Massachusetts where Larry attended seminary. Two more daughters, Kaelyn and Anna, were added to their family, and I traveled to Massachusetts after each birth to help care for the newborn. Leaving always brought sadness that I would not be near them to see their first smile or watch them take their first step. I never knew when I would see them again.

Even more difficult was not knowing how I'd be able to contribute to my grandchildren's spiritual growth. I knew they were in good care with their parents, but I also knew there was so much I could impart to them—if I just could be with them.

"Hi, Bam-ma. I wuv you!" said the tiny voice on my answering machine. I'd often receive phone messages that only made my longings more intense. I'd leave the messages on my machine to replay just so I could hear their dear little voices.

Before long, Larry called to confirm the news. "Well, Mom, it's official. I'll be taking that pastor position in Maine."

With a heavy heart, I drove to the seminary campus in Massachusetts to care for my granddaughters while Larry and Jennifer packed. Tears flowed as they pulled away to head north to Maine while I headed south to New Jersey.

A few weeks later I noticed a large bruise on my husband, Joel's, arm. "That doesn't look good. You'd better have that checked out," I urged.

"I'll call the doctor and make an appointment," he assured me.

After Joel's visit, the doctor scheduled some tests at the Cancer Institute of New Jersey. Joel was diagnosed with "hairy-cell leukemia," a rare but curable cancer. Joel would need chemotherapy immediately. It rocked our world to the core.

My next two summers were spent visiting my husband in the hospital while he endured chemotherapy then caring for him while he recuperated at home. Guilt was my constant companion reminding me of how much I longed to be on vacation in Maine. The financial drain and emotional strain brought on by Joel's cancer exhausted both of us. Making trips to Maine was certainly out of the question.

There was so much I wanted to share with my granddaughters, especially things concerning the Lord. I wanted them to know the goodness and faithfulness of God, even in our difficult circumstances. My son told me that the girls included healing for Grandpa in their nightly prayers. *Lord,* I prayed, *my heart is breaking! Please make a way for me to see my family.*

Then one day the words of a newscaster caught my attention: "Pretty soon you'll be able to talk to someone and see them on your computer at the same time." He sounded like someone from another planet. *How would that be possible? How would we be able to see someone on our computer screen?* I didn't understand it, but I knew it was an answer to my prayer.

Not long afterwards, I was speaking to a friend whose son and family are serving as missionaries to Paraguay. "I Skype with my grandchildren," she reported.

"Skype? What's that?" I asked ignorantly.

Right away, I called my son in Maine to set up an appointment to Skype. My brother's Christmas gift to me—a webcam—made my wish come true. Before I knew it, three squealing granddaughters were shoving each other aside for a seat in front of the camera so they could talk with Grandma. I don't know if they saw the tears in my eyes as we shared that first call.

During our first visit, Adrienne, age ten, played her piano recital piece for me. She danced around the room in delight. Kaelyn, age seven, jumped up and down with excitement as she told me what she was learning in school. The youngest, Anna, age six, kept peering into the computer screen as if she was trying to figure out how Grandma got in there! Then Grandpa entered the room to join our conversation.

"Hi, Grandpa," they all chimed.

They saw that Joel looked good. There was visible evidence that the Lord was hearing all our prayers, especially mine for how to impart Jesus to them from across the miles. Together we sang Sunday school songs, making hand motions to "This Little Light of Mine" and "Jesus Loves Me." Overwhelmed, I rejoiced in the Lord, "I don't know how this is possible, Jesus, but I'm grateful!"

I took full advantage of this wonderful new technology to stay as close to my grandchildren as possible. I read them Bible stories over the computer, prayed with them and for them, and shared with them my journey of faith in the Lord—all the things I had longed to do since they were babies.

Sometime later, Larry and Jennifer needed to head to the West Coast and asked if I could babysit while they were gone. When I pulled into their driveway, the girls ran out as fast as they could. They warmed up to me right away—all because of Skyping.

During my visit, Kaelyn motioned for me to come near her. As I leaned over, she whispered in my ear, "Grandma, I prayed in my heart today and asked Jesus to come in."

I could hardly contain my excitement. "Oh, Kaelyn! That's wonderful! Grandma is so happy. We'll tell Mommy and Daddy as soon as they get back from their trip." It was such a privilege to be present when my granddaughter asked Jesus into her heart. I was grateful that technology had brought us close enough in our relationship that she wanted to share her news with me.

We've experienced numerous subsequent visits over the internet. This past Christmas was especially meaningful. During our visit, I watched as each child took an ornament off the tree and explained that it was their "Baby's First Christmas" ornament. They were thrilled to show me the handmade ornaments that I had never seen. Then Anna brought her "Children's Book of Christmas Carols" to the computer to sing. All three of them shared with me the "Birthday Party for Jesus" they attended. I listened intently as they played the piano and sang duets. I was thrilled that they could see my delight as I clapped after each performance.

Skyping has changed our lives, and we like the change! Knowing that I'm just a call away from seeing (not just hearing) my grandchildren is comforting. I can enjoy their happy faces and know that they are thriving physically and spiritually. They often share stories of their own young faith journeys with me, and I can't help but think that being able to tell them my stories has somehow helped them grow in the Lord.

As we end our visits, I remind them to "Keep reading your Bibles, keep going to church, and keep loving Jesus." They always respond in unison, "We will, Grandma!" After our "good-byes" and "I love you's," Anna extends her arms, hugs the computer, and whispers, "I'm hugging you, Grandma!"

And I blow her a kiss good night.

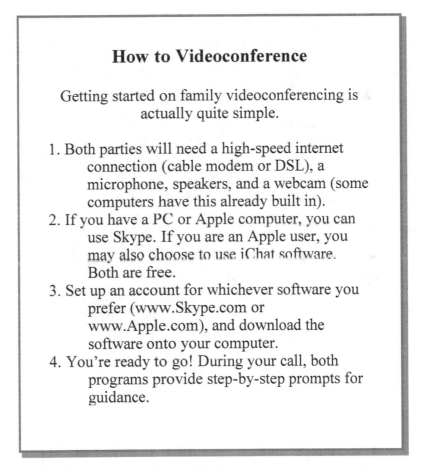

How to Videoconference

Getting started on family videoconferencing is actually quite simple.

1. Both parties will need a high-speed internet connection (cable modem or DSL), a microphone, speakers, and a webcam (some computers have this already built in).
2. If you have a PC or Apple computer, you can use Skype. If you are an Apple user, you may also choose to use iChat software. Both are free.
3. Set up an account for whichever software you prefer (www.Skype.com or www.Apple.com), and download the software onto your computer.
4. You're ready to go! During your call, both programs provide step-by-step prompts for guidance.

Grandparents in the Bible

Salmon and Rahab: Grandparents of Obed

"Salmon the father of Boaz, whose mother was Rahab, Boaz the father of Obed, whose mother was Ruth, Obed the father of Jesse" (Matthew 1:5).

Both "outsiders," the prostitute Rahab and the foreigner Ruth, were married into the family of Abraham's descendants and the bloodline of Christ. God welcomes into His family, and uses for His good purposes, any person whose heart is tender toward Him, regardless of their family name or where they come from. No matter what your family may look like to you, He can use you and your family for His good purposes, too.

Points to Ponder

- Even though Grandma was not happy about her son's family moving, she told her son, "I'll support you wherever the Lord leads." Knowing your kids are following God makes this easier to do, but even then it can be difficult. How have you shown support for your kids or grandkids in the past even though you weren't happy about their decisions? What situations are they facing right now where they really need your support? If you feel you can't support them for some reason, how can you gain the necessary strength from God to do so?

- This grandmother was heartbroken when she learned that her grandchildren were about to move even further away from her. Most devastating to her "was not knowing how I'd be able to contribute to my grandchildren's spiritual growth." What do you find most difficult about having your grandchild live far away? How have you coped with this challenge? How can you encourage others who may be facing a similar challenge?

- For this grandmother, Skyping has changed her relationship with her grandkids in many ways—all for the better. She's even been able to help them grow spiritually because of their Skyping conversations. What tool do you currently use to stay connected with your grandchild that you believe has significantly improved your relationship with him? If you haven't found such a tool yet, what steps can you take to begin researching and trying to find one?

➢ Grandma sees Skype as an answer to her cry to God for helping her be able to connect with her grandkids. How has God answered your prayers of staying connected with your long-distance grandchild? What prayers do you believe are still waiting to be answered? Take a moment to lift those requests to God again, and listen for His quiet voice of guidance.

➢ When Joel was sick, the grandparents were not able to visit their grandkids at all. If you're in a situation that prohibits you from visiting your grandchild, what is the best way you've found to regularly correspond with him to help reinforce your relationship and help influence him for the Lord? What are some other creative ways you can reach out to him to draw him even closer to you and God?

Steps to Take

1. Make it a point to connect with other grandparents of long-distance grandchildren. This can be done in person or even through online grandparenting forums and blogs. Encourage each other by sharing ideas and tips of how to stay connected with your family and how to help your grandkids grow in Christ even though you're miles apart.

2. Do you feel challenged by technology? Do you know the difference between a text and a tweet? To keep in touch with your long-distance grandchild, it's helpful to be technologically savvy. If necessary, enroll in a community college course or library workshop to learn about email, social networking, and videoconferencing. It's a great way to stay involved in your grandchild's life!

3. When your grandchild comes to visit, be sure to take lots of pictures of your time together. Once he's gone, take time to create a scrapbook or online photo album of his visit and send it to him. Having these photo memories of you with him will help reinforce the bond you share.

Scriptures to Study

"Hope deferred makes the heart sick, but a longing fulfilled is a tree of life" (Proverbs 13:12).

❖ When our deepest desires remain unfulfilled, we tend to become discouraged and give up hope. As soon as those desires materialize, we are instantly re-energized and brought back to life! Don't allow the seasons of being separated from your grandchild send you into despair. God knows right where you are, and in His timing, your longing will be fulfilled.

"I long to see you, so that I may be filled with joy" (2 Timothy 1:4).

❖ Paul was experiencing the hardship of separation from a loved one when he wrote this heartfelt letter to Timothy. Seeing how Timothy had grown in the Lord because of Paul's mentoring caused Paul great joy. Rejoice in those times you can see your grandchild, even if you can only "see" him on a screen from miles away. Praise God for technology that enables us to connect with and minister to others halfway around the world.

"Praise be to the God and Father of our Lord Jesus Christ, the Father of compassion and the God of all comfort, who comforts us in all our troubles, so that we can comfort those in any trouble with the comfort we ourselves have received from God" (2 Corinthians 1:3–4).

❖ If you suffer from not being able to spend time with your long-distance grandchild, know that God sympathizes with you. Take your burden to Him, and rely on the Holy Spirit in you to bring you the comfort you need. Use this season of your life to bring comfort to others who may be going through the same struggles you are, and point them to the God of all comfort as well.

One Way to Pray

Dear Lord, I know that You see my struggle and know how difficult it is to have my family live so far away. I thank You that You provide comfort and strength when I need it most. I ask that You would help me to find ways to connect with my grandchild over the miles, even if it means that I need to learn how to use some high-tech gadgets! Help me to be supportive of my family, regardless of whether or not I agree with their choices. Do not allow me to be a stumbling block that hinders them from drawing closer to You.
In Jesus' name. Amen.

Prayers, Notes, or Ideas

_____

_____

_____

_____

_____

_____

_____

_____

_____

Chapter 9

Grandparenting Across the Pond
by Kristin Lee Taylor*

The British call the Atlantic Ocean the "Pond." Two of my grandchildren, Brianna and Joy, live in London. Saying, "They live across the Pond" makes it seem like they're not so far away. And, in reality, the physical distance of over 5,000 miles away isn't our biggest concern.

My son, Rob, was brought up in church, stayed active in our church youth group, and served by playing the piano occasionally in our church services. But when he went away to college he became entangled in the secularism that permeates so many college campuses. After college, Rob took a job in Hollywood, once again surrounding himself with people who rejected any form of Christianity. In time, Rob married a Jewish girl. At first, he tried to avoid the conflict between Christianity and Judaism by simply ignoring both religions, but as time went on he completely deserted Christianity.

My daughter-in-law, Terri, is one of the sweetest and most thoughtful people I know, as well as being a wonderful wife and mother. Unfortunately, she too, has abandoned her religious roots and therefore provides no spiritual impact to her children.

Due to airfare costs, my husband and I can only visit London once a year. That doesn't leave much time to try to fill the spiritual void inside our precious little granddaughters. Trying to make the best of the time we have, I make it a point to always bring Christian children's books with me. I write Christian books for kids, so I'll bring my own books as well as those of my author friends. I strategically choose books that talk about God, not Jesus, so I won't offend my Jewish daughter-in-law. I feel as though I'm always walking a tight rope, balancing teaching the girls about the Lord without stepping on the toes of their parents. My greatest fear is that Rob and Terri might forbid me to continue.

A regular prayer of mine has always been for

Hope for Hollywood

Do you know someone working or living in Hollywood, or do you have a heart for helping others escape the secularism of the entertainment industry? In recent years, there has been an explosion of Christian ministries, resources, and prayer groups in and for Hollywood. Here are just a few organizations you may want to connect with:

• **www.HollywoodPrayerNetwork.org** – Provides regular prayer needs and accepts prayer requests for working professionals in Hollywood
• **www.ActOneProgram.com** –Trains Christians to write for and work in Hollywood as missionaries to Hollywood, the most influential mission field on earth
• **www.168project.com** –Challenges and trains Christians to write and produce short films based on God's Word
• **www.A-E-M.org** –A ministry focused on the arts and entertainment
• **www.MovieGuide.org** –Reviews and discusses movies from a Christian perspective

wisdom on how to move Brianna, age five, and Joy, age three, into a deeper level in their spirituality besides just reading Christian books. I so desired for them to learn to pray to Jesus. I wanted desperately for them to begin seeing Him as a good friend—someone they could count on in times of need as well as talk to every day, about everything. My opportunity came when our London family visited Southern California for a family wedding.

After the wedding, Rob and Terri flew to Seattle for business, so Dave and I had a divine appointment alone with our granddaughters for four days. One of Brianna's first questions was, "Can we go for a ride in the caravan?" The British call our fifth-wheel trailer a "caravan."

"Yes, we will take you and Joy camping at Dana Point State Beach," I assured her. "We'll camp in our trailer right on the beach. You can build sandcastles and play in the waves if the water's not too cold."

Without wasting any time, we quickly loaded the trailer and headed for the beach. The kids were thrilled with all the new sights and the upcoming prospects of roasting hot dogs and hamburgers! After a full day and full stomachs, we ended our first night with gooey, chocolate-ty smores. This was the girls' first camping experience, and they could hardly contain their excitement.

When it grew too cold to remain outside, we retreated into the trailer. Brianna looked around puzzled and finally asked, "Where are we going to sleep, Grandpa?"

Keeping a straight face, Dave replied, "On the table."

"On the table?" she asked with widened eyes. "That's too hard!"

Chuckling, Dave showed her how the table magically turned into a comfy bed with cushions. A look of relief swept across Brianna's face.

Every night during our campout, we read stories from a Bible storybook and then discussed them, making sure the girls understood the importance of the stories and the lessons learned. We also made it a point to pray with and for the girls before going to sleep each night. Dave and I did what we could to use the little time we had together to introduce Brianna and Joy to Jesus.

One day I picked up the girls' cousins who live close by and brought them back to play at the beach with us. After an exhausting day, I put my granddaughters (and my tired husband) to bed then drove the girls' cousins back home. Upon returning to the trailer, I discovered that Brianna had read the entire remainder of the Bible storybook on her own. My heart skipped a beat!

By the time the girls went back to London, they were saying their own prayers every night and were looking forward to our nightly Bible story. I prayed that the memories of our time together and the spiritual disciplines they learned would stick with them long after leaving California.

I've found the best way for us to stay in touch with our granddaughters while we're apart is through Skype. The girls love that we can actually see each other through the camera attached to our computers. During our "visits," I'll usually read stories to the girls, although I have to be careful, because their mother is always nearby.

I have an entire bookcase of children's books, and I'll choose ones based on the Old Testament to read on Skype. Two of Joy's favorites are *Leo, the Littlest Lion* and *The Humpy Grumpy Camel*. Leo is about a baby lion that is in the lion's den with Daniel. He prays that Daniel will be saved. The camel story is about Joshua marching around Jericho.

One day I had just finished reading *Leo, the Littlest Lion* to Joy. I heard Terri call from the kitchen, "Girls, dinner is ready." Joy immediately said, "I'm going to un-Skype you now, Grandma. Goodbye." Click. I turned to Dave and said, "I've been un-Skyped, and I didn't even know that was a word!"

I treasure the time I can spend talking to my granddaughters on Skype. I truly believe God has used this technology in our family to increase the depth of our relationship with each other.

Once when I was talking to Joy on Skype, she asked, "When are you coming to visit?"

Already knowing my travel plans, I replied, "In February."

The next time I spoke to her was a couple of weeks later. Her opening comment to me was, "Grandma, it's February!"

I said, "It is. And we're coming to London in ten days."

Her eyes sparkled as she clapped her hands and announced in her British accent, "Oh, we'll have a sleepover and fix oatmeal with raisins for breakfast."

"Yes, Joy. In fact, we will have seventeen sleepovers."

The days passed quickly, and soon we were on a jet crossing the Pond on our way to London. I wondered if the girls would remember any of the things we had taught them at the beach almost six months before.

Keeping Christian Teens Christian

In the book, *Already Gone: Why Your Kids Will Quit Church and What You Can Do to Stop It,* Ken Ham and Britt Beemer explain why over 60 percent of twenty-somethings who grew up in a Christian environment are no longer walking with God. After surveying 1,000 youths who regularly attended evangelical churches through their teen years, Ham and Beemer discovered that these kids were not adequately taught basic apologetics. As middle-schoolers, they began having doubts about God and His Word. The best thing we can do for our youth is to provide them with solid biblical training and be prepared to immediately address any doubts they have concerning their faith.

Brianna was now six, and Joy was four-and-a-half and just beginning to read. I brought with me an eight-book series of early readers that I had written about four zany characters and their adventures. Susie is the narrator, and whenever the friends get into crazy situations, Susie prays. At the end of each book is a parable of Jesus, written on a young child's level. The child can see how the adventures of Susie and her friends parallel one of the parables of Jesus.

I was excited to discover that the girls loved the books! During our stay, Rob and Terri worked long hours, so I offered to give their nanny a break by putting the girls to bed. This gave me an opportunity to read one or two books to them each night. After reading, we once again prayed together.

One night Joy's face lit up in understanding. She said, "Susie prays just like Leo does."

I replied, "Yes, Joy, and just like you and I do."

I've come to learn that God will use the smallest things we give Him to work with to turn a heart His way.

Grandparents in the Bible

Obed: Grandfather of King David

"Obed the father of Jesse, and Jesse the father of King David" (Matthew 1:5-6).

Did Obed and his son, Jesse, have any idea what God would do through David? God's plans are glorious beyond what we can imagine, and He uses ordinary people like you and me to accomplish His plans. So don't despair if you don't notice any standouts in your family. There just may be a King David in your family line waiting to arise!

Points to Ponder

➤ This grandmother tries to be strategic with the precious little time she has with her grandkids. In what ways can you better prepare for visits with your long-distance grandchildren so you can influence them spiritually?

➤ When Grandma, Grandpa, and their grandchildren were camping at the beach, one of the grandparents' goals was to teach the kids spiritual disciplines they could continue once they went home. What are some simple, age-appropriate spiritual lessons or disciplines that you could share to keep your grandchildren engaged with God when they leave you?

➤ Grandma says, "I feel as though I'm always walking a tight rope, balancing teaching the girls about the Lord without stepping on the toes of their parents." This challenge is further compounded by the distance between them. The grandmother came up with a creative solution, which was to teach her grandkids from the Old Testament. In what ways can you compromise or reach an agreement with your grandchildren's parents when it comes to teaching them about the Lord?

➤ If you only get to see your long-distance grandchildren once a year—or even more infrequently—what are some creative ways that you could still communicate with them that could help them grow spiritually?

➤ A desire of this grandmother's was to teach her grandchildren how to see Jesus as a friend. In what ways are you able to demonstrate this to your grandkids when you're together? What are some practical ways that you can encourage your grandkids to have this kind of relationship with Jesus?

Steps to Take

1. Plan ahead for your next time together with your grandchildren. What resources can you have on hand, what activities can you plan, what places can you go that will help you make the most of your short time together by bringing them closer to God?

2. Write out the ways in which you may be walking on a tightrope between your child and grandchildren. If you're able, speak to your child about these issues and try to reach a compromise. If not, speak to the Lord and ask Him for ideas of how you can still influence your grandchildren without overstepping your boundaries.

3. Research and make a list of various resources, such as children's books, Bible story DVDs or audio books, and Bible computer games that you could send to your long-distance grandchildren to help them grow in their relationship with God. Ask them to bring their favorites with them when they visit so you can share them together—then perhaps you can shop with them for new additions!

Scriptures to Study

"Be very careful, then, how you live—not as unwise but as wise, making the most of every opportunity, because the days are evil. Therefore do not be foolish, but understand what the Lord's will is" (Ephesians 5:15–17).

❖ This world's evil forces continually pull at us—and at our children and grandchildren. It's up to us grandparents to make the most of every opportunity we have with our grandkids, especially if we don't get to see them often. Each time you are together with your grandchildren, be sure to ask the Lord what His will is for that particular visit. He may have steps for you to take in your seed planting that will result in a great harvest.

"I no longer call you servants, because a servant does not know his master's business. Instead, I have called you friends, for everything that I learned from my Father I have made known to you" (John 15:15).

❖ Jesus wants to be our friend. He wants to have the kind of relationship with you, and with your grandkids, that you would have with your closest friend. It was a great desire of the grandmother in this story that her grandchildren came to know Jesus as a friend and were able to talk to Him every day about anything. Do you currently have this kind of relationship with Jesus? Do your grandkids? If you answered no to either question, what steps can you take to be able to say yes?

"If it is possible, as far as it depends on you, live at peace with everyone" (Romans 12:18).

* ❖ This grandmother did not want to disrupt the peace in her family by overstepping her boundaries with her grandkids. Her solution was to present God's Word in a way that would not offend her daughter-in-law. Sometimes it is more helpful to promote peace than our faith. When we make a way for peace, God can make a way for our faith.

One Way to Pray

Thank You, Jesus, for helping me with the challenges of grandparenting from afar. Although I don't get to see my grandkids often, I ask that You help me make our time together count for eternity. Enable me, too, to create a peaceful balance with my grandchildren's parents so that I can openly share Jesus with my grandchildren. Thank You for helping the moments that I do get to share with my grandkids become some of the most memorable and precious of their lives. I pray that my grandchildren would come to know You as a very special Friend, one who sticks closer to them than a brother. In Jesus' name. Amen.

Prayers, Notes, or Ideas

_____

_____

_____

_____

_____

_____

_____

_____

Chapter 10

I Like Jesus!
by Peggy J. Cunningham

As missionaries in Bolivia, South America, my husband and I are immersed in a different culture and a different language, but Jesus is still the same. Our daily goal is to show His likeness, not ours, and to become more like Him daily. Our grandkids are just beginning this journey, and we have the challenge of planting seeds in little hearts far away, helping them to become like Him every chance we get. One time my granddaughter saw another likeness in me when she came to visit.

Payton was only three when our grandchildren came to Bolivia one Christmas, but even she experienced the frustration of learning a new language. Her big brother and sister were in a dual-immersion school in California and were able to communicate well in Spanish, their second language. They easily interacted with the Bolivian children, but not Payton. With big blue eyes and white-blonde hair, she immediately connected with me, her Grammie, in a unique way. It was obvious that even when speaking English, there was difficulty communicating with a child who was still learning her first language.

"Grammie," she exclaimed one day, "I like you!" Well, who wouldn't melt at that?

"Honey, I like you too," I replied, giving her a big hug and holding back tears of joy.

"No," she emphatically answered, placing clenched fists on her hips. "I like you!" Each word came from her lips slowly and deliberately.

Again, "I like you, too, sweetie," was my patient reply.

Then with frustration in her little voice, she yanked her long ponytail over her head and pointed to my hair. "I like you!" she tried again. I finally got it. Her whitish hair and mine were the same color; she was identifying with me as her "Grammie." In her mind, if she looked like me, she was like me. Her eyes twinkled in relief when she saw that I finally understood her.

I was blessed that she saw our physical similarities, but could she see Jesus in me as well? I needed to know how I could impact my grandkids' lives so they would be like Him. Psalm 17:15 states, "And I—in righteousness I will see your face; when I awake, I will be satisfied with seeing your likeness." We will be like Him someday, but what about now, daily becoming more like Him? God used a child to wake me into the realization that I needed to become more involved in my grandkids' spiritual lives and to help them on their journey to become like Him.

Ben, our oldest grandchild—quiet, reserved, and thoughtful—identified with us in a different way, through our children's ministry. All three grandkids dug in and helped with our Christmas outreach for the needy children around us in the valley and in the mountain areas of the country. Because these children live far from civilization, high in the Andes Mountains, they never

At-Home Missionary Ideas

Ways to teach your grandchildren about persecuted Christians:

• *Open Doors—serving persecuted Christians worldwide:* **http://www.opendoors.org**
• *Open Doors in the USA:* **http://www.opendoorsusa.org**
• *Voice of the Martyrs:* **http://www.persecution.com**

Ways to help your grandchildren reach out to other children:

• *Angel Tree—providing Christmas gifts to the children of imprisoned parents:* **http://www.angeltree.org**
• *Compassion International— sponsor and correspond with children around the world:* **http://www.compassion.com**
Operation Christmas Child— provides Christmas gift boxes to children worldwide: **http://www.samaritanspurse. org**
World Vision—sponsor and correspond with children around the world: **http://worldvision.org**

receive Christmas gifts or have the opportunity to hear the Gospel. It was our mission to bring them both.

Although our grandchildren were small children themselves, they saw the needs of the less fortunate in the world, and it changed their hearts. One day just before Christmas, as we drove home through little villages where children lived in mud houses and played barefoot on the dirt roads, Ben was observing everything from the backseat. "Grammie," he asked quietly, "Can we give gifts to all the kids in every village?" I was touched witnessing the compassion of Jesus flowing through this young child.

All three grandkids joyfully helped wrap presents, bake cookies, and bag goodies for the big day. They even went with their Grampie and took gifts and the Good News into remote areas. They became mini-missionaries for Jesus! They soon were connected with our vision, and a heart for missions was planted. Kayla, our middle grandchild, indicated her desire to come back and work with us "forever" helping needy children and telling them about Jesus.

Soon it was time for our grandchildren to return home. It was hard to see our time together end, knowing there would be years between our next visit. The house was suddenly sad and empty, and most on my heart was how I could stay in touch and influence their lives for Jesus from Bolivia. Instead of "I like you, Grammie," I longed to hear instead, "I like Jesus"—loving Him, liking Him, becoming more like Him each day.

It was then that God gave me an idea to write stories for them about the animals they had come to know and love while visiting us. Each story had a tie-in to a biblical principle. It was a way for me to connect with them and teach them about God from a distance.

As they grew and changed, I asked God for new ways to connect with them and to reach their world. The answer He gave me was found in technology. Because I love to write for children, I began a new adventure with my grandkids. I started writing children's devotionals and drawing my grandkids into the writing circle with me. I send them to websites to read devotionals and look for Bible studies, and they help me research themes. They learn what I'm writing about, and it gets them into God's Word. We've created our own email account, and soon we'll put our thoughts on a blog to share with other children. Eventual plans include translating the blog into Spanish for our computer students in Bolivia.

No matter what ideas God gives me I want to stay available for Him to use me in their lives. When Kayla was only five years old, she spoke twelve words to me that will forever be etched in my heart. She bent down and picked a flower as we were saying good-bye before our return to Bolivia that year. "Here Grammie, this is for you," she said as she handed me the flower, "so you will never forget me." I made a promise to never forget them and always be in touch regardless of the miles between us.

Little Payton once made a profound statement when her mom told her we were going bowling in Bolivia. She gave her mom a puzzled look and said, "You mean they can do that in their world?" We do live in a different world from them, but really, whether we live close or far away, all grandparents live in a different world from their grandchildren in some way. It's up to us to find ways to connect those different worlds so that our grandkids can learn from our example of what Jesus is really like.

God will always give us the wisdom we need when we ask. In 1 Thessalonians 5:24 we're told, "The one who calls you is faithful and he will do it." God has been faithful to use our ministry to show our grandkids a lost world outside America. And He has been faithful to help them to reach their own community for Christ when they're back home in California.

I know it will be a continuous journey, trusting God for new ideas and plans as they grow into adults; but I know it's a journey I don't want to miss. When I look at those small replicas of us and see

Jesus shining through, those two different worlds melt into one. Right now we're pressing on to that day when we awake, finally, with His likeness, in His new world, where we will all be like Him forever, our journey finally over with no more distance between us. We'll all say, "I like Jesus," and we will actually be like Him.

Grandparents in the Bible

Jesse: Grandfather of Solomon

"David was the father of Solomon, whose mother had been Uriah's wife" (Matthew 1:6).

Solomon started out well in his walk with God but was drawn away later in life. A life of privilege and riches matter little in a person's relationship with the Lord. In God's workings, the richest can fall; the poorest can become king. But all who rely on God find His grace and help to affect others for Him.

Jesse and David both passed down a legacy of faith and godliness to Solomon. Jesse probably didn't live long enough to see Solomon's failures, but even if he did, could he have prevented them? Probably not. If you're seeing failures in your children or grandchildren, don't give up on them! Continue praying and know that God can still use them for His glory, just as He did with David and Solomon.

Points to Ponder

- What qualities do you see in your grandchildren that make them look like Jesus?

- How can you encourage them by communicating to them that they are becoming like Him?

- In what areas do you see your grandkids "looking like you"? Are you proud that they're imitating you in these areas? Why or why not?

- In what ways can you do a better job to ensure that you are reflecting the character of Christ to them?

- This grandmother used the time she had together with her long-distance grandkids to get them involved in her missionary service. You may not have an opportunity to take your grandchildren to the mission field, but how can you instill in them from home a heart for missions?

- What service or organizations could you get your grandkids involved in with you when you're together? What character traits would they learn from serving in such a capacity that would help them to become more like Jesus?

Steps to Take

1. Talk with your grandchildren about ways in which they can grow to look like Jesus (for example, being more patient or not getting jealous). Find scriptures that support one or two of these ways. Discuss the verses together to help your grandkids learn what God expects from us in each area. How can you help your grandchildren put each point into practice in their daily lives?

2. Connect with missionaries supported by your church. Encourage your grandkids to serve with you by corresponding with them, praying for them, and, when you're together, shopping for care packages to send to them. Have some fun researching the places where the missionaries are serving by discovering the culture, religions, and food of the area.

3. If your grandkids are old enough, consider starting a blog with them to share Jesus with other children around the world. If your grandkids are still young, team up with them to create cards for kids who need a touch of God's love and encouragement. (Your grandkids can illustrate the cards while you provide the text.) On your grandkids' next visit, take them with you to distribute the cards in a children's hospital or orphanage.

Scriptures to Study

"The Son is the radiance of God's glory and the exact representation of his being, sustaining all things by his powerful word" (Hebrews 1:3).

❖ As Jesus the Son reflects the Father in all things, we should reflect Jesus in all things. As we do, those around us, including our grandchildren, will see Jesus in us and will therefore know what the Father is like. And isn't this why we're here: to know the Father and to make Him known to others? Think of the ways in which you are—and aren't—reflecting Jesus to those around you right now.

"Dear friends, now we are children of God, and what we will be has not yet been made known. But we know that when he appears, we shall be like him, for we shall see him as he is" (1 John 3:2).

❖ How we all desire for our children—and grandchildren—to be imitators of the good in us. We love to hear how our next generations have inherited our better qualities. It's no different with God. As His children, He wants nothing more than for us to become just like Him. And one day we will. But until then we need to allow Him to continue to change us into His likeness. This change happens the more time we spend with Him.

"[Jesus] said to them, 'Go into all the world and preach the good news to all creation'" (Mark 16:15).

❖ If you long for your grandkids to have a heart for those around them, you need to model to them how to share God's love and compassion. There are many ways we can "go into all the world" and many forms of "preach[ing] the good news." Help your grandchildren discover how and where they like to serve, and provide an example for them by allowing them to serve with you.

One Way to Pray

Precious Jesus, how I long for my grandchildren to be changed into the likeness of You. Show me how I can better reflect Your righteousness in all I do so that when they see me they also see You. Help me to teach them how to serve You by serving others and reaching out to those around them with Your love and mercy. I ask that You give them a heart for those all over the world who do not yet know You or who may be living in dire circumstances. And, give me creative ways to involve my grandkids in serving others when we're together. In Jesus' name. Amen.

Prayers, Notes, or Ideas

_____

_____

_____

_____

_____

_____

_____

_____

_____

PART 3

The Challenge of Non-Traditional Families

Life sure hasn't turned out as you expected. You watched as your child went through a divorce. Now she's a single parent and needs your help. Or you watched the romance bud and your child married someone who already had kids—instant family! Instant grandchildren! Maybe your child and his or her spouse opted for adoption and brought a child, or more than one child, who needed parents (and grandparents!), into their family.

Or maybe it wasn't adoption in your case. Maybe your child is one of those awesome people who takes in foster children. They desperately need the love of you and your child, but they also bring their own issues and struggles into their new family—issues you never imagined you'd have to deal with. They're not your flesh and blood, but it doesn't matter. You absolutely love these grandchildren. Who wouldn't? Or at the very least, God has placed a love for them in your heart and an urgency in your spirit to reach them for Christ. It's just a far cry from the usual bloodline family you assumed you'd have. And this difference may have introduced cultures, situations, or possibly even problems you never saw coming.

Or it could be you. You suddenly found yourself single—maybe divorced; maybe widowed. And then you found someone new to love, to pass through life with. And so you're remarried, and now you're trying to win the hearts of your new step-grandchildren.

Divorce. Widowhood. Remarriage. Adoption. Foster families. Blended families are common today, but they can bring uncommon challenges. How do you negotiate these types of dilemmas?

You long to reach out in love. To help. To support. To make an impact for Christ on your grandchildren, whether they are flesh and blood or not. But when your love isn't accepted, what then? When the spouse of your child is causing problems, is a threat, or is nowhere to be found, how can you intervene? Or should you? How can you straddle that fence of helping but not imposing? Or when you find you're competing for the minds and hearts of your grandchildren with the draws of the world, how do you get into the competition?

You know you're not alone. Many families have faced similar situations. Even in the Bible, we see the family struggles: Sarah and Isaac conflicting with Hagar and Ishmael (Genesis 21:8–10). Joseph's eleven brothers selling him into slavery (Genesis 37:12–28). And we see relationships where there is no bloodline become closer than blood, such as the apostle Paul writing, "To Timothy my true son in the faith" (1 Timothy 1:2). Blended families are nothing new. Nor are the unique challenges they present.

But they are new to you. So how do you find your way through the maze?

In the following stories, you'll witness great family challenges and grandparents overcoming them to influence their grandchildren for Christ. You'll read how one grandmother and grandfather helped their adopted daughter and granddaughter escape an abusive relationship. Then you'll watch another grandmother step in to help when her daughter's ex-husband is arrested for child abuse, but then her daughter's extended absences for business leaves her grandson angry and bitter.

You'll watch grandparents negotiate the practical difficulties of a blended family that combines different ages and ethnicities of grandchildren, and the challenges of finding ways to influence them all across, and in spite of, these differences.

You'll meet a grandmother who saw the worldly influences competing for her foster granddaughter and determined to have equal time for God. And finally, you'll meet a grandmother who remarried following her first husband's death and faced the challenge of winning over an angry new adult granddaughter.

No matter what your family challenges, you will find hope and inspiration for your situation. You will see how these grandparents relied on God's promises and His Word and found ways to impart knowledge of Him to the grandchildren He placed in their lives. You'll be amazed as God works out situations in ways these grandparents could never foresee—simply because they desired to teach their grandchild about God. And you'll be challenged to implement their ideas, or be inspired to find some of your own, to reach your very own grandchildren for Christ.

Chapter 11

Won by Love
by Christina Carmichael*

"Don't come near her, she doesn't like new people," Shannon said matter-of-factly as I walked toward her to pet her dog.

This was the first time I met Shannon, who at the time was in her early twenties. I had come to her father's house for a family member's birthday celebration. I wasn't sure what to expect as Shannon stood in defiance in the middle of the room holding her dog tightly in her arms.

To everyone's surprise, the dog jumped out of Shannon's arms and into mine. "Wow," I stammered as I stumbled backward.

"She likes you!" Shannon said with total surprise as the dog licked my face.

Eighteen months ago, I remarried after the death of my first husband. While David and I dated, I met six of his grandchildren but was a bit nervous about the seventh whom I didn't meet until a few months before the wedding. David told me that after the death of his first wife, Shannon had become quite an angry girl. I saw that immediately when I met her.

Shannon had lived with her grandparents after her parents' divorce, and she and her grandmother had been extremely close. Unfortunately, her grandmother, Alice, died of Lou Gehrig's disease,

After Alice's death, Shannon, then fifteen, rebelled against everything she'd been taught, would disappear for months at a time, no longer went to church, and couldn't even keep a job. If she was hired, she'd either quit almost immediately or get fired in just a few weeks. Because she didn't work, she didn't have a place to live. All she could do is stay with friends and relatives until they grew tired of her and asked her to leave.

Shannon was not at all happy that her grandfather was about to re-marry. After that first visit, there were some days it seemed Shannon accepted me and then other days when she wouldn't even talk to me when I saw her. I prayed for her to not only accept me but also to get over her anger at her grandmother's death. I especially prayed that she would find peace in Jesus.

One time I asked her, "Shannon, would you like to stay at my home for about two weeks and take care of my dog so I can visit my kids and introduce your grandfather to them?"

"Sure," she replied. "Can I use the swimming pool?"

"Of course."

Before David and I left home, I added, "Please don't have any friends over while I'm gone."

"No problem," she answered.

We returned a day ahead of schedule, and I was shocked when I walked through my home. She'd definitely had people over; the evidence was everywhere, including signs of smoking pot.

"I was here all by myself," she insisted. "The sheets are on the couches because I felt safer sleeping in the living room than in the bedroom."

"Two sets?" I asked. She looked at me in silence.

"Also, the day bed in my office has been slept in," I said calmly.

"I wanted to watch a movie on my computer, and the room was cold so I got under the covers."

I knew this wasn't true because whenever she stayed over, she watched movies on her computer in the guest bedroom, not in the office. Shortly thereafter, the neighbors confirmed that she'd had several overnight guests.

Discussing the issue again wouldn't get me anywhere, so I bit my tongue and just prayed. My hope was that by spending more time with Shannon, whom I'd come to love despite her lies, it would help her learn to trust me and to be honest with me and her grandfather.

One day, a month before the wedding, I asked her, "Would you like to help me find the perfect wedding dress?" I knew what I wanted—a fancy blue dress with a jacket.

"That sounds like fun!" she said and sounded surprised. We not only shopped, but I took her out to lunch where she told me some of the stories of her young life. Many of them were about her grandmother, which I was happy to listen to.

While we shopped, Shannon took me into some teen clothing stores, which did not have any appropriate dresses for a sixty-something-year-old grandmother. Finally, she took me into the perfect store, and we found a wonderful dress—long and blue with a jacket—exactly what I wanted. I was especially thrilled since I hadn't told Shannon what type of dress I was looking for. I hugged her, and she hugged me back.

As she grew closer to me, I asked her, "Would you like to go to church with us this Sunday?"

"Sure, I'd love to," she answered. However, when the time came, the outfit she wore was not appropriate for church—or any place else. However, we took her with us and tried to ignore the strange glances many in the church threw our way.

I wondered if she had done this to embarrass us, or perhaps to defy the church. I had hoped she didn't notice the looks. She did. "There's no way I'll ever go back to that church," she informed me the next time I invited her.

> ### An Encouraging Word
>
> *"We have to pray with our eyes on God, not on the difficulties."*
> (Oswald Chambers)
>
> *"Men may spurn our appeals, reject our message, oppose our arguments, despise our persons, but they are helpless against our prayers."*
> (Sidlow Baxter)

After the wedding, Shannon brought some friends around to meet her grandfather and me. I was thrilled the way she introduced me to one young man. "I'd like you to meet my new grandmother," she said, with a hint of pride.

I beamed at my husband. She had accepted me.

Shannon stayed with her grandfather and me again and often swam and used the spa. One night we had the whole family over to celebrate her birthday.

"Oh, by the way, the spa is hot," Shannon mentioned to me.

"When do you plan to use it?" I asked in wonder.

"Oh, I turned it on early this afternoon. I have a date and want to use it when I get back around 4:00 a.m."

"It only takes about an hour to get hot. Don't you think that's an awful long time to have it on?" I immediately thought about the high electric bill she generated.

I tried to explain this to her, but she wouldn't listen so her grandfather spoke with her. That didn't work either. Shannon packed her small amount of possessions and disappeared. I knew all I could do was pray for her. She appeared miserable as she constantly tried to have everything her own way.

I soon discovered that I missed her even more than I missed my own grandchildren who were out of state. Shannon made one quick phone call on my birthday to wish me a happy day but refused to talk any longer.

When she returned six months later, I hugged her and she hugged me back as though we'd just seen each other a day or two before. She was smart enough not to ask if she could stay with us again; David would not have allowed it.

She called us once to ask if we could take her to the doctor, as her car wasn't running. We did, and later we went to lunch. I asked her, "We've found a house we want to buy and wondered if you'd like to help us pack." I didn't expect she would.

But instead, she replied, "I've packed so often, I'm an expert at it. I'll be glad to help you."

Her grandfather invited Shannon to stay for a few days, and she and I talked often. She told me more memories of her grandmother and about some of the men she'd known in her life.

Then one evening she came in from outside quite upset. She sobbed as I held her and I told her, "I love you, Shannon."

She replied through her sobs. "I love you, too."

Gradually, her sobs slowed down. I didn't ask her what was wrong. I knew if she wanted me to know she'd tell me.

Later, while packing, David came across his first wife's Bible and journals. "What should I do with these?" he asked. We decided they would make a great gift for Shannon.

I glanced through the Bible and saw she'd written many notes—not only on the pages of the Bible, but on slips of paper tucked by various verses.

To surprise Shannon, we put all of the journals in a large fancy box for her to keep. As I packed them into the box, I prayed that God would speak to her through His Word and her grandmother's thoughts.

"Oh, Christie," she cried as she opened the box. "Thank you, thank you, thank you! I remember when Grandma wrote in her journals every day." She wiped the tears from her eyes and grabbed me. She hugged me so tightly I thought I might not be able to breathe; but that was okay.

I continue to pray for Shannon. She is not as angry as she was when we met, and she definitely dresses more modestly. More importantly, she reads the Bible and the journals we gave her.

Just as I have won Shannon over with my love, I have every confidence that one day God will win her over with His.

Grandparents in the Bible

King David: Grandfather of Rehoboam

Under Rehoboam's leadership, David's kingdom of Israel split into two with Rehoboam becoming king of Judah in the south, which included Jerusalem, and Jeroboam becoming king of the northern ten tribes called Israel. "There was continual warfare between Rehoboam and Jeroboam … And Abijah his son succeeded him as king" (1 Kings 14:30–31).

Just two generations from the great King David, the kingdom begins to fall apart. No generation can rely on the faith of previous generations. We each must be diligent in our own personal faith in God. Only then will we own it and have it to hand down to the next generation.

Points to Ponder

> ➤ Shannon's anger and rebellion appear to be rooted in the death of her grandmother Alice. There are many reasons why children, teens, and young adults act out, and sometimes the root cause of their behavior remains hidden from view. If you're dealing with any form of rebellion in your grandchild, what do you perceive the root of that rebellion to be? How is it hindering your grandchild's relationship with you? with others? with God?

> ➤ Throughout this story, God showed Christina how His hand was at work in helping her reach Shannon: having Shannon's dog, who doesn't like anyone, immediately jump into her arms; allowing Shannon to find the exact wedding dress Christina was looking for; opening Shannon's heart to want to help Christina pack for her move; and so forth. What "God winks" have you experienced that let you know He is helping you reach your grandchild? How can you stay more attuned to these occasions?

> ➤ When Christina invited Shannon to church, she went, but dressed very inappropriately. Do you think Shannon did this innocently, or on purpose to get a reaction out of Christina? How did Christina respond in this situation? How do you respond when your grandchildren push your buttons—

whether on purpose or not? Do you believe you respond in a godly manner? If not, what can you do to change that?

➢ In many ways, Shannon's behavior was a cry for attention and healing. She needed to feel valued as a person and confident that she could succeed in life. How did Christina help her in these areas? What can you do to help your grandchildren gain needed confidence and feel valued?

➢ Perhaps one of the best things Christina and David did for Shannon was give her Alice's Bible and journals. What meaningful, tangible gift might you be able to give to your grandchild that would help bring her closer to you and God?

Steps to Take

1. Think of things you can invite your grandchild to do with you, even though you may have very different interests or tastes. Grandma worked hard to include Shannon in mundane tasks like shopping and packing for a move. Even if what you're doing isn't exciting, it can show your grandchild that you're trying to reach out to her.

2. If there is a particular behavior or attitude that's hindering your relationship with your grandchild, go to God's Word to see how to handle it His way. Ask God for one specific thing you can do to overcome this behavior or attitude with His love.

3. Try to talk heart to heart with your grandchild to determine what the root cause of any ungodly behavior might be. Tackle this root issue with prayer and, if necessary, with godly counseling.

Scriptures to Study

"If your brother sins against you, go and show him his fault, just between the two of you. If he listens to you, you have won your brother over" (Matthew 18:15).

❖ If you are dealing with any form of anger, bitterness, or rebellion with any of your grandchildren, it's best to keep matters between the two of you. Normally, the situation will only grow worse if your grandchild thinks that you are criticizing him or her openly to others. How can you respectfully "show him his fault, just between the two of you" that may help to win him over?

"You have heard that it was said, 'Love your neighbor and hate your enemy.' But I tell you: Love your enemies and pray for those who persecute you, that you may be sons of your Father in heaven. He causes his sun to rise on the evil and the good, and sends rain on the righteous and the unrighteous. If you love those who love you, what reward will you get? Are not even the tax collectors doing that? And if you greet only your brothers, what are you doing more than others? Do not even pagans do that? Be perfect, therefore, as your heavenly Father is perfect" (Matthew 5:43–48).

❖ Hopefully, your grandchildren don't hate you, but there may be times when they certainly seem like enemies. These are the times when they need your love more than ever! When they see you respond to them in love instead of criticism or withdrawal, they'll begin to get a glimpse of what God's love looks like. What are some areas where you believe you need to continue reaching out to your grandkids in love, even when they act like an enemy?

"Do not be overcome by evil, but overcome evil with good" (Romans 12:21).

❖ The grandmother in this story had many opportunities to allow Shannon's behavior to overcome any chance they had for a relationship. But instead of allowing that to happen, the grandmother aggressively fought Shannon's behavior with acts of kindness and God's love. In what areas of your life have you witnessed goodness overcoming evil? How can you make this principle apply to your relationship with your grandchildren?

One Way to Pray

Father God, I know that relationships can sometimes become strained, especially among family members. As I try to work within our current family structure and make an impact on my grandkids, I ask that You show me ways that I can effectively demonstrate Your love to them, regardless of their behavior or feelings toward me. Help me to look past their disrespectful or ungodly actions and behavior to their hearts, so that I may have compassion and mercy on them. Draw them close to You by Your mercy and grace each and every day. In Jesus' name. Amen.

Prayers, Notes, or Ideas

_____

_____

_____

_____

_____

_____

_____

_____

_____

Chapter 12

Long Journey Home
by Paula Freeman

Impatient, I hovered near the phone. When would he call? What was happening? Unleashed, my imagination conjured up innumerable tragedies since my husband flew out that morning to rescue our daughter and granddaughter from an abusive situation some 1,200 miles away.

What a difference a day makes! Was it only yesterday she called? "Mom, I'm ready to leave and come home. I can't take this anymore!"

I desperately wanted to believe her. We had travelled this road just last year, only to lose her to a pleading phone call and a paid train ticket back. How could we know it would be different this time? Yes, she felt ready to escape. No, she hadn't told him she was leaving. She feared for her daughter's safety and clung to secrecy's protection. Discrete phone calls flew back and forth through the night as our plan unfolded. We quickly purchased plane tickets, secured a rental car, reserved a hotel room, and coached her through the final hours of this eighteen-month nightmare. I prayed God would give her strength to stick with her decision.

"I've got them, and we're on our way home," my husband finally reported. "Here, I'll let you talk to her." Seconds later, my daughter's voice drifted over the line. I listened, imagining how it must feel to flee with only a garbage bag full of clothes. No good-byes. No one knowing of her plans to leave. I admired her courage but wondered what our merging futures held as the three of them began their long journey home.

The starting place of our emerging reality stretched across twenty-three years and thousands of miles to a young woman who delivered her first child in a small Indian village; two days later, she died. Her baby soon appeared on the doorsteps of a foundling home, cocooned in tattered clothes, alone in the world. "I'm afraid she's too small to make it," the visiting doctor said, sadly shaking his head after examining her emaciated body. "Perhaps with your care she has a chance," he added, almost as an afterthought, to Vasantha, her aging caretaker.

Nine months later, we arrived to adopt our daughter. "For three months, day and night, I prayed God would save this baby," said Vasantha, wildly shaking her fist to punctuate the point. Her fervent words pierced my heart as she and I shared a tearful farewell and began our own long journey home.

Through years of growing up in a large, boisterous family, she simultaneously adapted to living with a deep, abiding sadness and loneliness whose cancerous tentacles wove themselves into her soul. Friendships gained importance, yet proved difficult to keep. Schoolwork suffered. Peer pressure triggered anxiety and stress. Life always felt shallow for my daughter.

"Sweetheart," I implored, "I don't understand why you won't continue with counseling if you know you'll come out whole on the other side. You won't be alone. We're here to walk this journey with you."

"I know, Mom," she said, tears streaming down her face. "It's just too painful."

We watched helplessly as she made poor choices and turned her back on God. When old enough to move out, she did. We felt rejected. Her six siblings were confused. None of us, however, was surprised when she revealed she was pregnant. "We've decided to get married and move back to Ohio and live with his parents," she announced flatly one day.

Conflict ensued. Her husband remained jobless and possessive. Her world grew smaller as her belly swelled. Trapped, she knew she had made one of the biggest mistakes of her life. Energy and hope drained from my daughter like the last gulp of water down a hungry drain. I anguished over the life that my granddaughter appeared doomed to live. I felt desperate, with prayer as my only recourse.

"God, I will be involved in my granddaughter's life any way You ask. Please just help them out of this situation," I bargained.

He was about to take me up on that offer, even as I entertained second thoughts. Having an adult child and grandchild move home collided with my plan for my life. Resentment oozed into crevices created by crumbling dreams of an empty nest. Up to this point, being a grandparent included sending our grandsons home to their parents after a fun day or overnight stay. But no longer, because ready or not, here they come!

Creating a Safe Family Meeting Environment

- *Always open and close in prayer, allowing the Holy Spirit to guide your time together*
- *Keep all criticisms constructive and offer possible solutions for every problem*
- *Balance every negative comment with a positive, encouraging one*
- *Be transparent and vulnerable*
- *Listen attentively to each family member's opinions and comments*
- *Close the meeting on a positive note, offering specific steps to be implemented before the next meeting*

It's now been over a year since our daughter and granddaughter returned home to live with us. I struggled at first, feeling grouchy and impatient. What happened to my life? Slowly, I'm learning to grieve my losses and embrace my new reality. Daily I try to implement the great exchange … God's plan for mine. I now have an opportunity to impact one little girl's life in ways I could never imagine. While our empty-nester friends plot their next trip and sink into retirement, we're dusting off booster chairs and making room in the car for a car seat.

Although God accepted my offer, He provided the grace to navigate relational landmines and conflicting expectations as our families merged.

"Mom, I appreciate what you and Dad are doing to help me and Sophie," my daughter explained one afternoon, "but I don't want to feel like a kid in your home again. I have my own ideas about how I want to live my life and raise my daughter."

"That's great," I said. "I really don't want to raise more children; you're her mom. I think we're just going to have to figure out a way to blend our two families and come up with appropriate boundaries and expectations. What would you think about holding some sort of family meeting each week where we can talk things out?"

"Well, maybe," she said, "if you promise not to get mad at some of the things I may want to share."

"I think I can handle that. Let's give it a try. We can share about our week and discuss some issues we might be dealing with … what do you think?"

"OK. I guess it could work," she said reluctantly.

Some meetings were short, simple, and straightforward. Others involved more serious issues, tense moments, and tears. We did, however, begin to arrive at a healthy living arrangement that blended our two families.

And Sophie? She first arrived at our doorstep sad, withdrawn, and irritable. We grieved for her early months and knew healing would take time. "Father, You knit Sophie together in her mother's womb," we prayed. "You know the person You created her to be. Help us to see that too. You know what she's experienced and how her heart's been wounded. You are the Great Physician and the Mighty Counselor. Please help us help Sophie. Protect her and draw her to Yourself."

As weeks melted into months, we witnessed a depressed baby blossom into a delightful little girl whose saucy personality and contagious sense of humor mocks her earlier self. She's learned to walk, feed herself, begin to talk, and generally wiggle her way into our lives and hearts in unbelievable ways.

Saying grace at shared family dinners became a cornerstone of our busy lives. At first she reluctantly held our hands and watched, baffled by this strange ritual. As weeks passed, she began to bow her head, mimicking others around the table.

"Pray, pray!" she now insists as we gather, wiggling the fingers of her outstretched hands, inviting them to be held.

"Amen!" she soon squeals, thrusting her hands upward, expecting others to share her delight.

Knowing the importance of healthy physical touch, we look for ways to affectionately love her. Her stressed-out countenance has relaxed with a consistent daily routine. Taking time to play and read with her, listen to her, and pray for her all express our Father's love and point her to Jesus. We've grown to view this season as a time to prepare the ground, to sow seeds we pray will yield a tender, believing heart. We now possess the hard-earned wisdom of knowing how quickly time passes and how unimportant most of life's distractions can become.

Sophie's dad is missing in action; his choice. Her Bum (our grandkids' name for their grandpa) has become a most-important person in her life, second only to her mom. Each evening before bedtime, they sneak into the family room to share a juicy orange or dance to Christian music—a special time to nourish both their souls. We pray God will replace her father's absence with His presence … and right now, that looks and feels a lot like her Bum!

Our daughter's homecoming launched a positive cycle for her and Sophie. She returned to school and secured a job, while participating in counseling and growing into a nurturing mother. Most importantly, however, she's attending church with a body of believers who support her in this new season. "This is the first church home I've truly felt loved and accepted in," she recently shared. "And I want Sophie to grow up going to church too!" We're learning the Lord knows delightful short cuts on that long journey home when His arms are the destination.

Grandparents in the Bible

Rehoboam and Maacah: Grandparents of Asa

"Because Rehoboam humbled himself, the LORD's anger turned from him, and he was not totally destroyed. Indeed, there was some good in Judah" (2 Chronicles 12:12). Rehoboam's son Abijah succeeded him as king, and Abijah's son, Asa, succeeded Abijah as king of the kingdom of Judah in the south. "Asa did what was right in the eyes of the LORD, as his father David had done … Asa's heart was fully committed to the LORD all his life" (1 Kings 15:11, 14).

Although some generations might turn from God, He sees to it that the legacy of faith will never completely die out. Take heart and know that God can draw individuals to Himself in spite of the mistakes of previous generations.

Points to Ponder

➤ Paula could look back on her daughter's childhood and see the struggles she faced and the pit of depression she had fallen into. What do you think may've prevented her daughter from going down the path she chose for herself? If you were in Paula's position, what would you've done to try to rescue her daughter? What obstacles are currently preventing you from being able to help your child or grandchild follow the right path for their lives?

➤ Paula made a deal with God in exchange for His help with her daughter and granddaughter, promising, "I will be involved in my granddaughter's life any way You ask." God will always take us up on such promises! Have you made a similar promise to God regarding your grandchild? If so, are you holding up your end of the deal? Are you willing to make such a sacrifice if necessary? If not, why not?

➤ Paula navigated relational landmines and conflicting expectations by introducing family meetings. What landmines do you see, or possibly foresee in the future, that may pose problems in your relationship with your grandchild and his parents? If a family meeting won't work for your family, what other tool or event could you use to communicate family issues and boundaries?

➤ When Paula's daughter and granddaughter first came to live with her, she admitted that the new arrangement "collided with [her] plan for [her] life," caused her "resentment," and made her feel "grouchy and impatient." How has an unplanned or difficult family arrangement caused you to feel and respond? Paula worked daily to exchange God's plan for hers. How do you need to do the same?

➤ After Paula began investing into Sophie's life, she became acutely aware of how "quickly time passes and how unimportant most of life's distractions can become." What have you allowed to distract you from the important things in life? What steps can you take to get back on track with keeping first things first?

Steps to Take

1. Consider the various sacrifices you feel God is asking you to make for the sake of your grandchild. If you're struggling with any of these due to resentment, selfish motives, or a feeling of inadequacy, take them to God one by one. Ask Him to change your heart and empower you so that you're able to be obedient to all He's asking you to do.

2. Write down ideas for having regular family discussions concerning areas of disagreement, establishing boundaries, and so forth, with your child and perhaps grandchildren, if they are older. Share these ideas with your child to arrive at one that will work for both of you, and begin to implement it.

3. Talk to God about ways that you can begin to simplify your life and remove the distractions that are keeping you from being fully engaged in those things that are most important.

Scriptures to Study

"Do not be deceived: God cannot be mocked. A man reaps what he sows. … Let us not become weary in doing good, for at the proper time we will reap a harvest if we do not give up" (Galatians 6:7, 9).

- ❖ Don't ever think that the sacrifices you are making for your grandchildren are overlooked by God. Every prayer, every kind word, every act of kindness is a seed that will one day produce a mighty harvest of blessing in your life!

"[Jesus] himself bore our sins in his body on the tree, so that we might die to sins and live for righteousness; by his wounds you have been healed" (1 Peter 2:24). See also Isaiah 53:4–5.

- ❖ Jesus' death on the cross has made provision not only for physical healing but emotional as well. Paula's daughter and granddaughter both needed—and received— healing for their emotional wounds. God has already healed you and your family members through the death of His Son. It's yours— take it by faith!

"'Don't be afraid,' the prophet answered. 'Those who are with us are more than those who are with them.' And Elisha prayed, 'O LORD, open his eyes so he may see.' Then the LORD opened

the servant's eyes, and he looked and saw the hills full of horses and chariots of fire all around Elisha" (2 Kings 6:16–18).

❖ At times, we may feel as though we are surrounded by darkness and overwhelmed with discouragement. But we should take heart, because as long as we're walking with the Lord, there will always be more who are with us than we realize. God's army encamps around us! What circumstance are you facing that has you overwhelmed? Ask God to open your spiritual eyes to see who's in the battle with you.

One Way to Pray

I praise You, Lord, that You are the Great Physician and Mighty Counselor. You know the depths of the hurts and wounds that my children and grandchildren have experienced. Thank You for providing healing for any emotional or physical pain they are still dealing with, and for completely restoring them to Yourself. Show me what I can do to help expedite that healing and bring wholeness to our family. And thank You for Your daily grace enabling me to set aside my selfish desires to better reach out to my grandchildren. In Jesus' name. Amen.

Prayers, Notes, or Ideas

_____

_____

_____

_____

_____

_____

_____

_____

_____

Chapter 13

The Full Armor of God
by Grace Hewson*

"Kiss Mommy good-bye," I coaxed.

"I did at home. Just let her get out of here." Bobby never bothered to look up from the videogame he was playing.

My daughter's grey eyes flashed with anger while her body tensed. Within seconds, her eyes glossed over with tears. "See you in a few days, honey." She mustered an icy smile toward her son. "I'll call you later to say goodnight."

I waved good-bye from the car as Celina lugged her suitcase, laptop, and multiple bags through the double doors of the train station. All the while, I prayed silently that God would keep her safe. Bobby sat in the backseat, his fingers hitting the computer buttons like lightning strikes as his eyes remained focused on the screen.

Celina is now a single mom with sole custody of Bobby after the authorities found her ex-husband guilty of child abuse. Bobby has stayed with my husband and me on and off ever since. Our daughter gallantly pulled her and Bobby's broken lives together by putting herself through college, landing a job in her field, securing an apartment, and ultimately, beginning a new life. But with the upheaval in the economy, her job was terminated. After calling us in tears because she was unable to pay her rent, we told her to come home.

As soon as I put the car in gear to head home from the train station, I heard Bobby zip his case locking the Game Boy inside. "Grammy, can we play I Spy on the way home?" he asked happily.

Bobby's constantly shifting moods created a rough four days for us together. Like a rogue wave, searing emotions erupted before Celina left, crashing into our secure ship. I knew I was in for another battle. My fight was not a physical war but a spiritual battle with eternal consequences.

Although my daughter and I had established and agreed upon our parenting roles whenever she's away, the best-made intentions do not always work as planned. Celina breezed home expecting her six-year-old son to accept her hugs and gifts. Instead, Bobby's volatile emotions were coming to a head like the perfect storm. His agitation at his mother's absence as her work took her farther from parenthood could no longer be ignored.

"You're not my mom anymore," he yelled at my daughter one day. "Grammy does everything for me."

"I don't know why I bother coming home at all!" she screamed back.

We knew going into this joint-parenting journey that the lines of authority might become confused and blurred for a young child. Stress, hurt feelings, and exhaustion fed Celina's anxiety. She threw the proposal she was working on to the floor and geared up for a full-blown rant. Her ringing cell phone mercifully diffused her explosion before it began.

"Hi," she cooed, forgetting the entire encounter. "Yes, I can be back in town by midnight for that meeting we discussed." She disappeared up the stairs like a wraith. I knew we would not see her again until she had her bags packed.

Celina had found a new job that took her from the quiet country suburbs to the "wild frontier" of New York City. She was sure this was her ticket to a better life. But we were concerned for Bobby. He's in the first grade and has some learning difficulties. We knew making him change schools again and move to a place without a support system would be a disaster. Celina wisely chose to leave him with us until she found a suitable place to relocate. What we did not count on was how the lure of the Big Apple was going to affect all of our lives.

Initially, Celina was only to be gone for a few days at a time. But days have turned into weeks. The high demands of her job and the promise of future wealth constantly wrestle for her attention. Even when she is home, she leaves her heart and mind behind. "Grammy, don't leave me with her," Bobby often protests. "She talks on the phone the whole time."

My husband and I are walking a tightrope existence, not wanting to lose either of them to the fast-paced lifestyle that's quietly drawing Celina in. She was raised in church but began falling away after her husband abused Bobby. Now, the glamour and excitement of her new career completely overshadow her spiritual roots.

Until my daughter came back to those roots, I knew it would be up to my husband and me to teach our grandson about the Lord. Bobby has always had a wild imagination, and loves to play with swords, battle imaginary enemies, ride flying horses, and say magic words. I used these desires God had planted in his heart to teach him about the armor of God as discussed in Ephesians 6. Our first battle was against unforgiveness. After the abuse, I used the time to reaffirm him in the Word of God. We knew this issue was a key element to Bobby's emotional health.

We jumped around the kitchen like warriors, using our plastic swords and reciting Scripture. "I forgive people who hurt me because God forgives me," Bobby would say, flailing his sword over his head. We would pretend his sword burst into flames, knocking his enemy to the ground. I will never forget the joy I felt the day he came home from counseling with a tiny trinket to give his dad because he forgave him.

When he first moved in with us, he hated going to his Sunday school class and would cry and complain from the moment he woke up. At church, he insisted on staying in the service with me. In time, he progressed into his classroom but never had much to say about what he was learning. I decided to stop asking him about his class and just be ready for when he did want to talk.

It wasn't long before we started seeing fruit emerge in Bobby's life simply from attending Sunday school. One afternoon when I picked him up from the school bus stop, I found him talking a mile a minute to one of the older boys in the group. He abruptly left his friends and raced to the car. "Grammy," he began, completely out of breath. "Do you know that Bentley does not believe in Jesus and he never goes to church?" He looked at me wide-eyed, astonished by his discovery. "Do you think he can come with us on Sunday?" he asked.

My smile lit up the entire countryside.

As Bobby has progressed in understanding, I teach him Scripture verses that we recite daily. He enjoys knowing that his sword's power is increasing. Little did I know the third commandment would create a whirlwind!

His mom often uses words that would curl the hair of a sailor. One day Bobby called her out on this issue: "Grammy says we should say 'Sorry, God' when we say Jesus' name like that."

Celina was furious. "Mom, I don't want my son telling adults what to do. It's disrespectful! Besides, you're making him crazy with that stupid game. I don't want you teaching him about God."

I apologized to her yet remained solid in my conviction. "You know we are not to take the name of God in vain. Do you want

---

Armor of God Children's Resources

- *"Full Armor of God" game—Be the first to completely clothe your game card character in the full armor of God using peel-and-stick pieces of armor! For ages 4-8. (David C. Cook Ministries)*
- *Full Armor of God costume—Complete armor set made of molded, flexible plastic. Comes with parenting guide, including activities and scriptures. (David C. Cook Ministries)*
- The Armor of God: A Children's Bible Study in Ephesians 6:10–18— *Paperback by David Walters. Recommended for ages 6–12.*
- *Armor of God—16-page coloring book with stickers to help kids discover God's spiritual armor. (Standard Publishing)*

him to learn a 'do as I say not as I do' philosophy, or do you want to be a good role model?"

She was silent.

Reflecting on the past few days since Celina's been away, I see a tempest on the horizon. Sitting at home in my recliner with Bobby curled up beside me watching cartoons, our ship feels safe and secure. But I'm aware that a new enemy is brewing in my grandson's heart. I am preparing Scripture verses about anger to use during our sword fights.

I thank God that my husband and I have this opportunity to help Bobby work through these difficult emotions using prayer, love, and modeling forgiveness. It's a privilege to see the fruit of our efforts in Bobby's life, even though we know we still have a ways to go.

A ringing phone startled us away from the cartoons. "Hi Mom, can I speak to Bobby?" Celina sounded happy.

I handed the receiver to my grandson. "It's your mom."

"Tell her I'm too tired to talk now."

I felt her frustration through the phone. "Forget it," she said sharply. "I'll call him tomorrow."

She hung up before I had a chance to think or respond. I felt my own blood begin to boil, knowing that Bobby was once again acting out against her absence. If I've learned anything in this battle, it's to stay strong in faith yet be as gentle as a dove. We're navigating our lives through choppy waters, and we need to be alert to the pain our grandson and daughter may experience along the way.

God's Word and prayer are our most valuable weapons, and we must learn how to use them skillfully. It's time once again to wield my sword. But instead of a plastic one, I will pick up the mighty sword of the Spirit—the Word of God—and fight a spiritual adversary who has come to destroy this family. And I won't back down until he's defeated.

Grandparents in the Bible

Abijah: Grandfather of Jehoshaphat

Abijah raised a son, Asa, whose heart was fully committed to the Lord. And God was with Asa's son, Jehoshaphat, "because in his early years he walked in the ways his father David had followed … His heart was devoted to the ways of the LORD" (2 Chronicles 17:3, 6).

The training and love for God that Abijah passed on to Asa affected Abijah's grandson, Jehoshaphat. And the lives of these faithful men affected all the people of their nation, and beyond. The seeds of godly faith that you plant in your child and grandchild will one day be evident not only vertically, in generations to follow, but also horizontally, as they reach out to those around them.

Points to Ponder

➢ This grandmother recognized that her "fight was not a physical war but a spiritual battle with eternal consequences." It's sometimes easy to forget what Paul said to the Ephesians: "Our struggle is not against flesh and blood, but against the rulers, against the authorities, against the powers of this dark world and against the spiritual forces of evil in the heavenly realms" (6:12). But we must always keep in mind who our true enemy is.

Have you ever lost sight of the spiritual enemy you're fighting and started fighting the flesh and blood of your own family instead? Take a moment to ask God to help you recognize the devil's tactics when he begins to influence your child or grandchild and to help you stay focused on the real target of your battle.

➢ Grammy tapped into Bobby's wild imagination and love for swords and battling imaginary enemies to teach him a powerful truth about the armor of God. What are some fun and creative ways you can use your grandchild's passions to help him discover biblical truths or draw him closer to God?

➢ How did the grandmother in this story strategically use the spiritual discipline of Scripture memorization to help Bobby with specific issues he faced? How can you do the same with your grandchild? If your grandchild is too young to memorize and recite Scripture, how else can you plant God's Word into his heart?

➢ Grace was firmly stuck in the middle between Bobby and his mother. How was she able to achieve a successful balance of allowing Grace to live her life the way she chose, yet still stand solid on her biblical convictions, especially as they concerned Bobby?

If you're stuck in the middle with your child and grandchild, what lessons can you apply from this story that may help you achieve a successful balance?

➢ Bobby was acting out toward his mother because she was inattentive to him and often away from home. But his emotional wounds shouldn't excuse the disrespect he showed her. How can you help your grandchild adhere to the fifth commandment and honor his parents even when he has been hurt by them?

Steps to Take

1. Create your own armor pieces based on Ephesians 6 from cardboard or other sturdy material, or purchase them from a costume store. Have fun using these with your grandchild while you teach him the function of each piece according to Scripture.

2. Make a list of Scripture verses that address the various issues your grandchild may be facing. Work with your grandchild to understand and memorize these verses so he can use them as a sword to fight his spiritual battles. For quick reference, use a concordance or topical promise book to help locate scriptures.

3. Find out from your grandchild what he's most interested in or passionate about. Work with him to create fun ways of using those interests to learn about God and His Word.

Scriptures to Study

"Put on the full armor of God so that you can take your stand against the devil's schemes. For our struggle is not against flesh and blood, but against the rulers, against the authorities, against the powers of this dark world and against the spiritual forces of evil in the heavenly realms. Therefore put on the full armor of God, so that when the day of evil comes, you may be able to stand your ground, and after you have done everything, to stand. Stand firm then, with the belt of truth buckled around your waist, with the breastplate of righteousness in place, and with your feet fitted with the readiness that comes from the gospel of peace. In addition to all this, take up the shield of faith, with which you can extinguish all the flaming arrows of the evil one. Take the helmet of salvation and the sword of the Spirit, which is the word of God" (Ephesians 6:11–17).

❖ When we are fully clothed with God's armor, we're protected from any attack—deception, feelings of unworthiness, unbelief, fearful or evil thoughts—and we're equipped to fight back with God's Word. Teach your grandchildren to never go through their day without first putting on God's armor.

"Be self-controlled and alert. Your enemy the devil prowls around like a roaring lion looking for someone to devour" (1 Peter 5:8).

❖ The devil will always look for someone to devour, but that doesn't mean he will always find someone. What makes the difference in whom he finds? Those who are protected with God's armor and know how to fight him back with their faith in God's Word will not be devoured. When the devil prowls around your family, what will he find? How can you help protect your loved ones from his attack?

"Children, obey your parents in the Lord, for this is right. 'Honor your father and mother'—which is the first commandment with a promise—'that it may go well with you and that you may enjoy long life on the earth.' Fathers, do not exasperate your children; instead, bring them up in the training and instruction of the Lord" (Ephesians 6:1–4).

❖ Children—and grandchildren—need to be taught how to obey their parents in a godly manner. And they need to know that God Himself will reward them for it. But God also has instructions for parents and grandparents: We must not do things to cause our children to disobey or to frustrate them. When both children and parents do as God commands, families will operate in balance and harmony.

In what ways is your family out of harmony with one another? What specific things can you do according to these Scripture verses that would help promote family harmony?

One Way to Pray

Thank You, Father for the weapons that You've given us to fight the spiritual forces that come against us. Help me to always be aware of the spiritual battle I'm in and to never forget that my fight is not against other people, including my family! Show me the areas in which my grandchild needs me to help him fight enemies of fear, rejection, depression, or anything else that is causing emotional hurt in his life. Give my grandchild a deep desire for Your Word so that he can wield it as a mighty sword when he's feeling defeated. I pray too for creative ways to engage my grandchild in learning Your Word and how to abide in it. In Jesus' name. Amen.

Prayers, Notes, or Ideas

Chapter 14

Let Them Come
by Anne Agovino as told to Elsi Dodge

"Why don't you come stay with us until you find a job and get settled?"

Though our daughter Karen wanted to be independent, she was quickly realizing she simply couldn't do it all on her own. Our invitation gave her the opportunity she needed to get her life together and raise her child in a safe setting. Becoming a single mother certainly wasn't planned, and I knew her repentance was real. It helped the adjustment process that her toddler, Hannah, loved her new day-care near our home and certainly enjoyed the triple parenting she received from her mom, her grandpa, and me. Because our adult children used the term "Grandma" for their own grandmother, I was called Nana by this precious, first grandchild.

I had accepted Christ at age sixteen but didn't experience real growth in my faith and relationship with Him until my two children were teenagers. That's when my husband, Frank, also became a Christian, and our children began their own journey with the Lord. Since we'd never had the chance to build a safe, nurturing Christian home for our own little ones, we looked forward to raising Hannah as part of God's family.

I never questioned Karen's faith, but she was restless, distracted by the temptations and necessities of growing up. She pulled awkward shifts at her new job, and time spent with friends kept her up late. She had a constant desire to sleep in, even on Sundays.

Frank and I prayed regularly for her, allowed her to have her space, and gladly established a routine of taking little Hannah to Sunday school and other church activities. We rejoiced in her developing faith and noticed her quick mind and deepening perception.

Karen grew too, settling down and eventually falling in love with a young man she met at the hospital where she worked as a nurse. A Christian man, we were glad to hear, though not particularly active in his faith. We easily accepted Donnell, an African-American, into our family, and we loved his sweet spirit and obvious love for our daughter. We prayed that blonde Hannah would not face prejudice in this blended family, as St. Louis is square on the Mason-Dixon Line.

Though I loved all of my grandchildren, my heart went out especially to Hannah, stuck at home every day all summer, watching television with two teenaged step-siblings. I had never considered taking only Hannah for special days out. After all, Hannah's new brother and sister were my grandchildren too. But the age range was wide, and I didn't want to undercut my daughter or cause trouble in this newly blended family. I decided to invite all three for a day at the Missouri Botanical Garden, a St. Louis must-see. This was simple for me to plan and something Hannah and I had often enjoyed.

"You want me to get up early to go see someone's *garden*?" fourteen-year-old Darryl asked, grumbling. I chuckled at his honest reaction.

All three kids loved the experience, including Darryl who flashed a contagious grin as he climbed trees and fed the "radical big fish!"

"Thanks, Nana! I love you!" Hannah called out to me from her porch when I took them home, hot, sweaty, and happy.

The following week we tried the Science Center, checking out the animatronic dinosaurs, Egyptian artifacts, and other "cool" collections. When I dropped the kids off that afternoon, twelve-year-old Dee ventured a soft, "Thanks, Nana."

Another week we sought respite from the St. Louis heat at the pool. "Way to go!" Dee shouted as I gave in to the temptation of the waterslide. "You're not a too-old Nana!" Thanks, I think.

We went on picnics, experimented with crafts, and played games. At Hannah's request, we had a sleepover at my house. Even Dee and Darryl got up without complaining when they smelled maple syrup and the bacon Grandpa was frying. As we got more comfortable with one another, I instituted what Dee called "Nana lectures," friendly suggestions about cooperation, choosing friends, and God's guidelines for marriage—all my attempt to plant godly seeds for the future. I knew they were listening, even when they groaned.

I wanted the kids to remember as much as possible of our fun summer months together, so I made a memory book for each of the children that included photos of each activity as well as a few of

Darryl's shots of animals we had seen. I knew they each enjoyed having the books to reflect on after our summer had faded away. I didn't realize the impact our time together had had, though, until our family Christmas celebration. Darryl pulled me aside and asked shyly, "Are we gonna get to do Nana Camp again next summer?"

"Well … sure!" I said. I hadn't been thinking as far ahead as summer, but apparently our time together had never left Darryl's mind. I liked thinking of our experiences as a camp.

When the following summer rolled around, we repeated our favorite activities from the previous year and found new places to go. I expanded my Nana lectures in response to heartfelt questions: "Nana, there's this guy in my class who keeps bugging me to smoke pot, what should I do?"; "Why do you like to go to church?"; and "How do you know when love is for real and forever, Nana?" I didn't know if these questions were being asked to their parents as well, but I was thrilled that I had this opportunity to share God's viewpoint on these important issues.

One day when Karen's family and my son, Brian's, family were both with me, Brian's oldest daughter—although still in preschool—overheard us talking about Nana Camp. "What about me?" complained Darby. "I want to go to Nana Camp, too!" My concern for Hannah had prompted me to begin Nana Camp (even though it didn't originally have an official name!), and, in the process I had become involved in the lives of Dee and Darryl as well. At the same time, I certainly didn't want to leave out Brian's three preschoolers. "Lord, help me know what to do!" I prayed in desperation.

I wish I could say He provided me with an organized plan. Instead, He showed me doors of opportunity and reminded me of His command for sharing His law and His love with children. Not just on special occasions, and not just taking them to church. I was to tell my grandchildren about my Savior in everything I did, every day.

When Hannah turned ten, I wanted to talk with her about the power of true beauty, modesty, purity, safe dating, and other pre-adolescent issues. I purchased a Christian book covering these topics, and Hannah and I carefully planned eight dates together, corresponding to the material. I was touched when, shopping for swimwear that June, Hannah commented, "I don't think you should get that one, Nana. The men will 'finish the picture,' you know, like we talked about from the book." Looking in the mirror, I saw her point, and thanked her.

I thought it best that Nana Camp would start when a child turns six, so Darby gladly joined us the following summer. During that school year, I took the preschoolers to the Bible Study Fellowship (BSF) program I was involved in. My husband had included Hannah and Darby in the elementary school classes during his evening BSF, and the girls complained when he chose not to continue in the fall.

"But, Grandpa, we like learning about the Bible!" Darby said.

"And we like having special time with you," Hannah added.

So Frank developed a home Bible study program for his girls, who called it Bible Study Grandpa (BSG). The year Darby's sister Sydney joined them, they studied the Gospel of John, taking different roles each week as they acted out the stories. Frank filmed the entire series, calling it "JOHN: The Movie," and showed it to the families at the end of the year. It was a bit tricky, with the actress playing Jesus changing in each scene, but we managed to figure it out. By the time the Bible study series had ended, the kids certainly knew all about that book!

"What will we do in Nana Camp this summer?" Darby, now ten, asked recently. "It'll be just me and Sydney and Hannah, right? 'Cause Aubrey's still too little, and Dee and Darryl are too busy."

I smiled, thinking about my varied grandchildren. Darryl's been playing football, and sings and writes rap music. At nineteen, he's considering his future: college? career? I pray my Nana-lectures and unconditional love continue to help guide him. I keep in touch with Dee as one of her Facebook "friends." A high school junior, her future plans are still quite fluid. I continue to pray for her, and she knows it.

Bible Study Fellowship

BSF began over fifty years ago as a small, home Bible study. Its 200,000 members now cover thirty-eight countries. BSF teaches various Bible topics for a period of thirty weeks throughout the year. They have classes for preschoolers through age seventeen that run concurrently with their adult classes.

Contact them via the website:
http://www.bsfinternational.org

Hannah's sister Kennedy is now two, and we recently welcomed another little sister, Meghann ("I like girls' names with double-Ns," my daughter told me). As I gazed into Meghann's dark eyes I couldn't help but think of the Nana Camps that await us.

"We *are* going to do Nana Camp, aren't we?" Darby persisted. "You're not ... you're not too old or anything, are you, Nana?"

"Me? Too old?" I laughed, and she joined me. "You'll just have to keep me young!"

"How can I do that?"

"Pray for me," I answered. "And keep teaching me fun games."

"Okay!" she giggled.

When I look at all my grandkids and consider the spiritual fruit that has come of our times together, there's no way I could stop now.

Grandparents in the Bible

Jehoshaphat: Grandfather of Ahaziah and Jehosheba; Great-grandfather of Joash

Jehoshaphat's son, Jehoram, succeeded him as king then, "put all his brothers to the sword" and "did evil in the eyes of the LORD" (2 Chronicles 21:1, 4, 6). After him, Jehoram's youngest son, Ahaziah, became king but was killed. His mother, Athaliah, usurped the throne and killed all the royal descendants, or so she thought. "Jehosheba, the daughter of King Jehoram, took Joash son of Ahaziah and stole him away from among the royal princes who were about to be murdered.

He remained hidden with them at the temple of God for six years while Athaliah ruled the land" (2 Chronicles 22:11). Then the priest, Jehoiada, revealed him, made him king at age seven (2 Chronicles 24:1), and put Athaliah to the sword. Joash lived for God until Jehoiada died, but then "abandoned the temple of the LORD, the God of their fathers." God sent Jehoiada's son, Zechariah, to warn him, but Joash ordered him stoned to death in the courtyard of the Lord's temple. Joash was murdered in his bed "for murdering the son of Jehoiada the priest" (2 Chronicles 24:25). His son Amaziah succeeded him as king.

Jehoshaphat knew God. His son Jehoram did evil. Joash, raised in the temple by the good priest Jehoiada, only lived for God as long as Jehoiada lived. Parents or grandparents who love and honor God, and had a good upbringing in the house of God, are important, but ultimately each individual chooses whether he or she will follow God … or not.

Points to Ponder

➤ When Anne's daughter came to live with her, she made three distinct choices as to how she was going to deal with Karen's walk with God: She never questioned her faith, she prayed for her regularly, and she gave Karen her space. In what ways do you believe this may've positively or negatively impacted Karen? Would you have taken such a hands-off position if you were Anne? Why or why not? If you're in this position currently, what approach have you chosen to take with your son or daughter?

➤ Why was it wise for Anne to make sure that all of the grandchildren were comfortable with one another before she began her "Nana Lectures"? In what ways have you taken time to build solid relationships with your family before trying to talk to them about God? What impact has this had?

➤ After the first summer of Nana Camp, Anne was able to use the kids' questions to launch her Nana Lectures. How have you been able to create an environment for open communication with your grandkids? What could you do to make them even more comfortable asking you questions and sharing their hearts with you?

➢ In response to God's leading, Anne looked for ways to tell her grandchildren about Jesus in everything she did, every day. Are you honestly doing the same? If not, what are some changes you can make in order to do so?

➢ When Frank planned not to return to BSF, his granddaughters complained because they wanted to continue going with him. What was Frank's creative response to their request for learning about the Bible? Would you be willing to do something similar to what Frank did to teach your grandkids about God's Word? What activity or program could you implement right now to help teach them?

Steps to Take

1. If your grandkids span a large age range, think of activities suitable for varying ages that you can enjoy with each other. Plan on doing these activities together on a monthly or bi-monthly basis to help build a relationship with all of your grandchildren.

2. What are some age or maturity milestones your grandkids have in their near futures? Plan special "dates" or one-on-one time with them to discuss the issues surrounding these milestones, to celebrate them, and to teach about God's plan for their lives during these special times.

3. Consider holding regularly scheduled, informal Bible studies with your grandkids. Research biblical themes or topics you'd like to share with your grandkids. Perhaps add a creative element as well, such as having the kids act out the story or make a relevant craft.

Scriptures to Study

"There is neither Jew nor Greek, slave nor free, male nor female, for you are all one in Christ Jesus" (Galatians 3:28).

❖ If you are a grandparent in a non-traditional or even blended family, you may have different races and cultures that are attempting to become one unit. Help make that transition easier by remembering that the most important thing is for everyone to become one in Christ. Look past the external appearances and labels, and keep Jesus at the foundation of all you do for your family.

"Accept one another, then, just as Christ accepted you, in order to bring praise to God" (Romans 15:7).

❖ Adjusting to family changes can be difficult. If you're having a hard time accepting certain members of your family, think of all those who Christ willingly accepts into His family. None of us is perfect, but in Christ, we are forever being changed into His likeness.

"Each one should use whatever gift he has received to serve others, faithfully administering God's grace in its various forms" (1 Peter 4:10).

❖ You may not have a gift for creating children's skits or even organizing a home Bible study like these grandparents did, but whatever gifts God has given you, use them freely and abundantly to help your grandkids get to know Jesus.

One Way to Pray

Dear Jesus, I ask that You would help our family become one, loving each other and accepting one another in Christ. Help me as a grandparent to do all I can to bring about unity within our diverse family. Give me creative ideas of how I can include my grandchildren of different ages, interests, and backgrounds in activities where we can strengthen our relationships with one another. I pray that my grandchildren would always feel comfortable discussing their triumphs as well as their difficulties with me so that I can use those opportunities to point them to You. Use me however You desire to share Your law and Your love with these grandchildren You have entrusted me with. In Jesus' name. Amen.

Prayers, Notes, or Ideas

_____

_____

_____

_____

_____

_____

_____

_____

Chapter 15

G & G Retreat
by Francine Duckworth

"Mother, I'm teaching summer school. Can Tanya fly to Colorado and stay with you for six weeks?" I had prayed for a chance to be with our fourteen-year-old foster granddaughter, Tanya. She was so excited about coming, but I wasn't sure if the timing would work because I had just signed up to teach at a migrant school for six weeks. I prayed for God to intervene so I could see her. He did, working out the times and circumstances necessary for her to be with us.

When Tanya came to live with Deborah and Dean, her foster parents, at the age of five, she asked Jesus to forgive her of her sins. She wanted to live for Jesus the best she knew how. She prayed for her mom to also give her life to Jesus.

But at fourteen, there was so much more out there than church, school, and parents. The innocence of being five was long gone. I prayed with Tanya and discussed how we needed to do more than just have devotions in the morning and evening. Together, we planned our first G and G Retreat—a granddaughter and grandmother weekend.

The retreat rules were simple: I got equal time with her. If we shopped for two hours, we also did things to feed our spirits for two hours. When she spent the evening with friends at a movie, I wanted to have an evening of discipleship training. I wanted to do something that would help Tanya on her spiritual journey and prepare her for her future and for heaven. I didn't want to only do things that benefitted her physically or financially here on earth.

After twenty years on the mission field, my husband and I had just returned to America. We had no money to have a retreat in the mountains or at a resort, so we had it right in our rural Colorado home.

I orchestrated a schedule for our weekend that included a time for devotions together; time by ourselves to read the Bible, pray, and journal; a time for service projects, such as maintaining the bulletin boards at the church where her grandpa pastors, preparing Sunday school materials, visiting teens, senior citizens, or playing with children.

We started the following morning with a devotional time and prayer. I could tell by the look on Tanya's face that she wasn't so sure if she would enjoy this weekend retreat. I did my best to make it interesting and fun. She desperately wanted to spend time with me but wasn't so sure that it was going to be a fun weekend—spending time with her grandmother instead of friends.

But as we read, sang, and prayed, she sensed God helping her with some issues that she had been struggling with for a long time. After she had finished with her own personal devotions, she came to me and said, "Look at this, Grandma. This verse helped me last year when I was going through some stuff at school." It was awesome to see how God had been speaking to her through His Word.

I tried to encourage more of this through journaling. Tanya and I would each read a scripture verse, write it in our journals, then ask God what He wanted us to learn from it. Once we received His direction, we would write down whatever thoughts He gave us.

We took turns choosing the scripture and daily devotional message we wanted to focus on. We diligently sought the Lord's direction when we prayed, worshipped, listened to songs, and asked what He would have us do for that particular weekend.

I kept praying and asking God, "How can we compete with the world and its alluring pleasures? How can we help teens today grow in the knowledge of our Lord Jesus Christ when everywhere they turn the world has something fun for them to do?"

"Time with God" Tote

To encourage your grandchild to spend quiet time with the Lord, give her a pretty tote bag or him a sporty backpack filled with the following:

- *Bible*
- *Notebook or journal*
- *Pen or pencil*
- *Bible highlighters*
- *Age-appropriate devotional book (optional)*
- *Note of encouragement from you!*

I told Tanya, "I'm not going to tell you it won't be fun if you sin and live for the devil, but the Bible says that the wages of sin is death."

After one of our weekends together, she would leave a note in the bathroom for me: "Grandma, look at this scripture—Jeremiah 29:11. 'I know the plans I have for you...'" When she came upstairs for breakfast, I would have a scripture written on a note card on her plate or on the table at the place where she sat.

It wasn't always easy to stay and pray when a friend wanted her to go shopping. And there were times we got discouraged when we stayed home and didn't feel like we heard anything from the Lord. Even so, we both felt it was important to keep to our schedule and remain steadfast in our efforts.

The six weeks seemed to evaporate. Suddenly she was back home; back to school and the world. I knew the devil was fighting for her soul. The world and its alluring pleasures took her on a path very far from the thoughts and ideas shared at our Granddaughter and Grandmother Retreat.

Years passed, and I prayed. When Tanya and I saw each other we would talk about the Lord and share scriptures, but never as much as we did when we had our retreat.

I felt terrible when I heard that she went back to California and stopped living her life for God.

Then one day, I was traveling when I got a call from Texas. "Grandma," she said, "I need to have a spiritual retreat with you." Tanya was now twenty-three years old. I was so thrilled to hear her voice and her request.

"Tanya, I fly into Denver at 11:00 Tuesday night," I said. "You can meet me at the airport. I will take you home, and we can do just that." In order for her to visit me, she'd have to ride a bus for nearly twenty-four hours then wait at the airport until my flight arrived. I didn't imagine she would go through all that. But, then again, she was the one calling to spend time with me, not her mother asking if I could watch her.

When I got to the airport, I was surprised to see that she was actually there. One look at her and I could tell that she was definitely ready for a Grandmother and Granddaughter Retreat.

The world had not kept its promises. She knew God would. The world had not loved her the way God had. The world had taken everything dear and true away from her. She needed a G and G Retreat to help her get back to the Lord and what she knew in her heart to be true. "Oh, Grandma, I made the biggest mistake in my life by moving to Texas and living with—" she began, explaining in detail how her life unraveled.

We started the next morning. She spent time with the Lord and asked Him to forgive her and help her live for Him once again. We read, we prayed, we knew God would answer every prayer. God is a merciful God. He forgave her. Now we needed His direction, wisdom, and guidance from His Word and His people.

We ate. We prayed. We slept. We read. We knew that almost ten years ago, God had met us here, and we needed Him to meet with us again.

The first Saturday she was here, she spent all day with a female youth pastor from a neighboring town who did her own mini-retreat with Tanya. When Tanya left Colorado, she was filled— emotionally, physically, and spiritually.

"Grandma, that summer I spent here when I was fourteen was my best summer ever," she told me. When I heard that, I knew the G and G Retreat had been just what she needed. I believe it was her best summer ever because together we focused on living for Jesus.

Recently Tanya called and I asked her about sharing her story here. "God has been so good to me," she said. "I want to help other young girls." Tanya is now solidly living for the Lord—all because of God's faithfulness at a mini-retreat in a rural town with a grandmother who knew what she needed most.

Grandparents in the Bible

Amaziah: Grandfather of Jotham

Amaziah "did what was right in the eyes of the LORD, but not wholeheartedly" (2 Chronicles 25:2). After a battle with the Edomites, Amaziah brought back the gods of the people of Seir and bowed down to them. The Lord was angry and Amaziah was later assassinated. "Then all the people of Judah took Uzziah, who was sixteen years old, and made him king in place of his father Amaziah … He did what was right in the eyes of the LORD … But after Uzziah became powerful, his pride led to his downfall. He was unfaithful to the LORD his God …" (2 Chronicles 26:1, 4, 16). Jotham, his son, succeeded him as king. Jotham "did what was right in the eyes of the LORD …" (2 Chronicles 27:2).

Like his father Amaziah, Uzziah was not whole-hearted toward the Lord. Jotham, however, did what was right in God's sight. An imperfect parent or grandparent does not ensure that a child or grandchild cannot or will not wholeheartedly honor God. Sometimes that grandchild will learn what not to do, as much as what to do, from the generations that went before him.

Points to Ponder

➢ What do you think of this grandmother wanting equal time with her granddaughter to teach her spiritual things and not just "things that benefitted her physically or financially here on earth"? Was this a good way to approach the time she had with her granddaughter? Why or why not? How might you try to get equal spiritual time with your grandchild?

➢ Grandma had orchestrated a rather rigorous schedule for the two of them during their retreat. If you don't happen to be quite as organized or planned as Grandma, how could you still incorporate the various spiritual disciplines into the time you have with your grandchild? Which disciplines would be most important for the two of you to focus on, and why?

➢ Tanya learned the importance of spending quiet time with God and listening for His voice. How can you help your grandchild learn how to be still in God's presence and hear from Him? How can you encourage your grandchild when she feels she can't hear from God?

➢ How did Grandma and Tanya use Scripture note cards to encourage each other? What are some creative, age-appropriate ways you can encourage your grandchild with God's Word?

➢ God was faithful to meet Tanya again, nearly ten years later, when she returned to His presence at her grandmother's house. In what ways—big or small—has God shown His faithfulness to your grandchild in her time of need? How do you need for Him to display His faithfulness now? Take a moment to thank Him for His past faithfulness, and renew your faith in Him for His ability to work in your grandchild's life.

Steps to Take

1. Take a moment to prepare for your grandchild's next visit. Think of ways you can incorporate time for helping your grandchild learn and practice various spiritual disciplines.

2. Get alone in a quiet place with your grandchild. Together, practice being still before the Lord. For little ones, start with only one to two minutes of quiet time then gradually add more time as the children's ages increase. Help them to learn to remove mental distractions and focus their thoughts on God. Talk about the thoughts or impressions that came to them during this time.

3. Begin the practice of exchanging Scripture note cards with your grandchild. If you live near your grandchild, leave them in her room or a lunchbox. If not, mail them to her once a week or so to let her know you're thinking of her and praying for her.

Scriptures to Study

"Be still and know that I am God" (Psalm 46:10).

❖ It seems that one of the hardest things to do as a Christian is to be still long enough to focus on and hear from God. This practice is even tougher for children, whose minds and bodies are constantly in motion! Ask God what you can to do encourage your grandchild in this very important spiritual discipline.

"Train a child in the way he should go, and when he is old he will not turn from it" (Proverbs 22:6).

❖ Although Tanya walked away from the Lord for a while, she eventually returned to Him because of the spiritual seeds her grandmother had planted in her at a young age. If your grandchild has taken a detour off God's path for her life, don't despair. Your prayers and early training will help her find her way back.

"'For I know the plans I have for you,' declares the LORD, 'plans to prosper you and not to harm you, plans to give you hope and a future. Then you will call on me and come and pray to me, and I will listen to you. You will seek me and find me when you seek me with all your heart'" (Jeremiah 29:11–13).

❖ Just like Tanya, we won't discover God's good plans for our future unless we seek God with all of our heart. He puts the ball in our court to make the first move toward Him. But once we do, He promises to not hold back anything He has for us.

One Way to Pray

Heavenly Father, thank You that You promise to draw close to us when we draw close to You. You desire that we seek you with everything we've got, always putting You first place in our lives. Put a hunger in my grandchild's heart to seek after You in this way so You may show her the wonderful future You have in store for her and guide her along the path You've already paved for her. I pray that she would always stay close to You, but even if she does make a choice to stray, I ask that the seeds I've planted in her life will bring her back to You. In Jesus' name. Amen.

Prayers, Notes, or Ideas

_____

_____

_____

_____

_____

_____

_____

_____

PART 4

The Challenge of
Partnering with Parents

Let's face it, you're blessed! Your child and his or her spouse know the Lord. Not only that, but they are raising your grandkids to know Him. Or maybe for some reason, they're not actively teaching their children about the Lord, but at least one or both of them are not opposing you as you do. But even with parents who are faithfully walking with the Lord, or parents who aren't in opposition to Him, you have a role to play. Your grandchildren still need you and your godly influence in their lives.

Maybe you can see clearly that your grandchild is struggling with an issue. Maybe it's something you recognize because you struggled with the same thing when you were his age. You want to come alongside his parents and help. How can you partner with his parents to help him?

Maybe you've found yourself smack dab in the middle of an emergency, and suddenly you have the grandkids all to yourself for an extended period of time. Or perhaps they're not living with you, but are very close by and your child needs you to help care for them. You have a good relationship with the parents, but still it's a fine line to walk. How do you partner with your grandchildren's parents without stepping over that line?

Maybe you long to simply take matters into your own hands, take the kids and raise them yourself. Or maybe you *don't* want to take matters—and the grandchildren—into your own hands! But you might have to. Either way, you long to improve their lives or their situation by teaching them about God, by making sure they know His promises that will help them no matter their situation. You want them to know the Bible stories that reveal so much about how God loves us and helps us and intervenes in our lives. And you want to have the pleasure of teaching them the things of the Lord, but you don't want to overstep your role as a grandparent.

You know the godly influence the generations can have on those who come after them. After all, those are some of the stories you know from the Bible! For example, stories such as how Ruth's faith blessed her mother-in-law, Naomi. And how Ruth was rewarded for her faith by becoming, with Boaz, the mother of Obed, the grandmother of Jesse, and so the great-grandmother of David (Ruth 4:13–22). And then there are those two great-partnering women who so influenced Timothy. Paul wrote, "I have been reminded of your sincere faith, which first lived in your grandmother Lois and in your mother Eunice and, I am persuaded, now lives in you also" (2 Timothy 1:5). You long to pass on the legacy of faith as our faithful spiritual ancestors did.

In the following stories, you'll see grandmothers and grandfathers doing just that. Watch as one grandmother experiences with her son and daughter-in-law the agony of losing a grandchild during pregnancy. Then wait with her for more than ten years to finally receive the grandchild she longed for, just to realize that her son and daughter-in-law are doing nothing to raise this precious child in the knowledge of the Lord! What can she do? What should she do?

And then there's the grandma-to-be whose nineteen-year-old adopted daughter is pregnant. With both the father and the mother of this coming grandchild couch-surfing from one friend's home to another and both battling mental illness, how can she possibly partner with these parents to make a difference in her grandchild's life? You'll discover how a grandmother provides a place of refuge and spiritual training for her grandchildren, especially her grandson, who is learning to deal with anger and frustration brought about by a tumultuous family environment. Finally, you'll meet two grandmothers who find unique ways to help their grandchildren rely on God and deal with issues they're struggling with.

Through all these stories, you'll be inspired and equipped to partner with the parents of your grandchildren and help nurture your grandkids in the knowledge of and relationships with the Lord. You may find yourself singing a little song of comfort. Or taking a trip to the petting zoo. Or helping a grandchild overcome fear. You'll discover how other grandparents have helped, and encouraged, and you'll find help and encouragement for your situation too.

Partner with the parents of your grandchildren, as our Father partners with us, to influence your grandchildren toward an everlasting relationship with Him.

Chapter 16

Worth the Wait
by Rhonda Rivers*

My son's voice sounded stressed over the phone. "Mom, Susan's in surgery. She started bleeding, and I brought her to the emergency room."

"I'm on my way, Todd."

Within minutes, I dashed out to the car where my husband, Gary, waited with the engine running. Panic welled up in my chest. This was Susan's first pregnancy, and she wasn't far along.

Gary drove while I tried to figure out exactly what went wrong. "If she had a miscarriage why is she still in surgery?"

For a fleeting second, I remembered how we both felt when we learned we were going to be grandparents. We had waited so long for this blessing. Now uncertainty gripped us as we rushed to our son's side.

Todd met us at the entrance to the emergency room. "The doctor told me she had a tubal pregnancy. There's an infection, and they're removing the ovary and who knows what else." Todd blinked away tears. "Mom … our baby didn't make it."

I hugged Todd. "I'm so sorry. We wanted this so much for you. Do all you can to hold onto your faith. Remember, none of this is a surprise to God. We just need to lean on His strength right now. How is Susan? Does she know about the baby?"

"No, and I don't know how to tell her. She lost a lot of blood. One of the doctors will check in with us as soon as she comes out of surgery."

Susan's physical wounds healed quickly, but her emotional wounds festered. She and Todd argued often as the months passed. Their marriage was in trouble. Todd took to working late to avoid coming home to an angry and complaining wife, while Susan constantly fought depression, overcome with feelings of loneliness and abandonment.

A year dragged by. Todd and Susan managed to stay together, with their marriage somehow even strengthening. I prayed for their relationship, but they didn't confide in me. One year after another passed until nearly ten years vanished. Todd and Susan grew closer but never spoke of having another child.

I had been in a Bible class where we were studying Psalm 37. Verse 4 leapt out at me and spoke to my heart: "Delight in the LORD and he will give you the desires of your heart." I paused to contemplate what God was saying to me through His Word. Then, without really thinking, I spoke words that unexpectedly turned prophetic, changing our future. "It's amazing what God does in our lives. He has given me more than I could have thought or imagined."

I shared with the women about my wonderful godly husband and many other blessings. "Really, I could go on forever. There are just too many to count. And if I ever did try to count them all, I would surely miss some."

Then after a pregnant pause, I continued. "The only thing, and I hate to even mention it, is that I don't have a grandchild. I would love to hold a grandbaby in my arms, but it doesn't look like that will ever happen." Then I quickly added, "But, I have plenty to thank God for already."

It seems I underestimated the strength and determination of my daughter-in-law. Unbeknownst to me, she and Todd had seen a fertility doctor. Almost a year to the day after that Bible study, my grandson, Kevin, was born.

My vision of this child growing up in the church as his father did was not realistic. Neither Todd nor Susan had any interest in attending church. Sadly, my son did not appreciate his childhood connection to church and family.

We invited them to church often, and they did go a couple of times. Then I got the idea of inviting them to church events so they could experience the love and fellowship of other believers outside of a regular service. They joined us for our church's Easter breakfast and Easter egg hunt. They came to Christmas gatherings. Todd even went to Promise Keepers with the men's group. But none of this resulted in a commitment to regularly be a part of a church.

In the meantime, Kevin grew quickly.

I had mentioned to Todd several times that he and Susan should start going to church. That suggestion was brushed off with their excuse of being too busy. I delicately related that going to church often relieves the pressures of the week, and that worshipping with others helps put life in the proper perspective.

"God works in mysterious ways," I said. "You never know what He'll use to help you."

And Todd agreed. It wasn't that they didn't believe, he assured me. They just weren't committed enough to make a change. I understood that their baby made a huge impact on their lifestyle, but I remember how much I needed church when Todd was a baby. I couldn't imagine dealing with all my stress *without* going to church!

"Lord, they need to be in church! Any church—it doesn't have to be ours!" I cried aloud to God one day in frustration. He gently rebuked my impatience with Psalm 27:14, "Wait for the LORD; be strong and take heart and wait for the LORD."

When Kevin was three, he came over to see Grammy for a few hours once a week. I decided since he wasn't going to church, I'd bring church to him. I read him Bible stories, and we watched animated Bible story movies. At the time, his attention span was two minutes, tops. His mind was a blank slate, and I wanted so badly to erase the worldly influences I saw creeping in.

When I realized that he didn't yet know the words to "Jesus Loves Me," I encouraged him to clap his hands and sing the words back to me. "Come on, Kevin, look at Grammy. Jesus loves me, this I know …"

He laughed and clapped, then laughed some more. Sweet and innocent, Kevin had no clue what we sang about, but I knew he'd have plenty of time to figure it out. A few hours a week was better than nothing, but I wasn't seeing much progress. Suddenly he was four, then five, then in preschool, and I saw him even less.

One day my son and I met for lunch, and I reminded him that when he was little he used to go to Sunday school. He nodded.

"Yeah, I remember having to rush around Sunday mornings to make it on time."

My heart ached. "Is that all you remember about Sunday school?"

"Pretty much."

"I guess I remember it differently." I launched into fond memories of Todd reciting memory verses and singing Bible songs. Visions of Christmas and Easter plays flashed through my mind.

"It doesn't matter, Mom." His tone was condescending. "We don't have time for church. You know we believe in God, but you don't have to go to church to be a Christian. We have issues with the organized church."

"Issues with the organized church? That sounds like an excuse to me."

When he stood, I knew I'd overstepped my boundaries.

"Lunch is over. I need to get back to work."

I reached toward him. "Todd, I'm sorry. I really didn't mean it like that."

He turned and looked me straight in the eye. "I'm pretty sure that's exactly how you meant it. I'm sick and tired of hearing what you think my family should be doing."

"Sit down for a moment," I said, politely but firmly. "Todd, does Kevin know the story of Adam and Eve?"

"Mom, he's five."

I touched his arm. "You knew it when you were five." I tapped the table with my forefinger. "Does Kevin know about

Noah's ark and how it saved the world? Does he know what it means whenever we see a rainbow appear in the sky?"

Todd's gaze dropped to the table.

I continued, reminding Todd of the Bible stories and songs he'd learned in Sunday school. "Does Kevin know that the story of Jonah and the whale is a true story about obedience and forgiveness? And what about baby Moses floating in the river? You knew the words to 'Jesus Loves Me' and a dozen other songs that comforted you in the night. You quoted Scripture."

Todd looked at me. "Yes, I guess I'd forgotten. I did memorize Scripture, and I remember the first one was 'God is love.'"

> ### *Scripture Memorization Tips for Kids*
>
> - *Focus on no more than one verse per week*
> - *Ensure your grandchild fully grasps a scripture's meaning before memorizing it*
> - *Look for teachable moments throughout the week to reinforce the scripture*
> - *At the end of each month, review all of the verses learned during that month*
> - *For an organized children's program that promotes Scripture memorization, check out AWANA at **http://awana.org/***

"You were three when you learned that one. Why would you rob your son of the richness of the Bible and Sunday school?"

I remained cautious in my conversation, knowing not to go too far. "He's not going to get what you got by sitting at home Sunday morning."

He shook his head and said softly, "I know, Mom, but life gets in the way."

"Your son is worth the effort. It was worth it for you."

Three weeks later Todd, Susan, and Kevin came to visit. We sat around the fireplace after dinner. Kevin snuggled next to me. His sweet little-boy face turned to mine, and he gazed up at me, smiling his biggest smile. "I'm a big boy now, Grammy. I go to Sunday school."

My spirit soared. *Lord, You always answer my prayers!* I felt my eyes well with tears as I leaned over to hug my grandson. "Your daddy went to Sunday school, too—a long time ago."

My eyes met Todd's across the room. His eyes were wet, too. I thought of how impatient I was for a grandchild when God was orchestrating His perfect timing all along. To see now how God used one little boy to bring a husband and wife back to Him, I'd say this grandson was definitely worth the wait.

Grandparents in the Bible

Uzziah: Father of Jotham; Grandfather of Ahaz

Ahaz succeed Jotham as king, and "unlike David his father, he did not do what was right in the eyes of the LORD" (2 Chronicles 28:1). Ahaz worshipped foreign gods, not the True God, and he sacrificed his sons in the fire (v. 3). "The LORD had humbled Judah because of Ahaz king of Israel, for he had promoted wickedness in Judah and had been most unfaithful to the LORD" (v. 19). Ahaz took items from God's temple and shut its doors (vs. 21, 24). His son, Hezekiah, succeeded him as king.

Although Jotham did what was right in God's sight, his son Ahaz was a very evil king and did a lot to lead God's people away from Him. We saw earlier that Jotham succeeded his father Uzziah as king because Uzziah's pride led him away from God. We don't know how much influence Uzziah had on his grandson, but the story may've been different for Ahaz if Uzziah had continued to follow God with all his heart.

Points to Ponder

➤ This grandmother tried to connect her son and daughter-in-law to other believers and the things of God by inviting them to events other than church services. What events can you invite your non-church-attending family to? What other ways can you woo your family back into God's family?

➤ Todd's excuse for not attending church was that "We don't have time for church ... you don't have to go to church to be a Christian. We have issues with the organized church." Having "issues" with the organized church has become a common justification for many Christians who no longer attend church. How would you've responded to Todd's comment? How can you express to your grandchildren the importance of being involved in a local body of believers?

➤ Because Kevin's parents didn't attend church, Grammy brought church to him. If you are in a similar situation, how can you bring church to your grandkids without overstepping your grandparenting role?

➤ This grandmother confronted her son regarding his unwillingness to go to church, even for Kevin's sake. In what areas might you need to "speak the truth in love" (Ephesians 4:15) to your grandchildren's parents? How can you do this in a way that won't challenge their authority as parents?

➢ This grandmother realized that God had perfect timing in the birth of her long-awaited grandson. How might things have been different for this family if Todd and Susan had a child earlier? What unanswered prayers are requiring your patience for God's perfect timing? How can you begin to trust in His timing and not yours?

Steps to Take

1. Make note of any events, such as concerts, holiday programs, or home-based Bible studies that your church or other churches in your area are hosting. Pray over these options, asking God which one(s) would be best to invite any non-church-attending family members to.

2. What are the weights that are holding back your grandchildren or their parents from having a closer walk with God—work? sports? entertainment? Consider talking to your family about these issues and suggesting ways to work around some of their obstacles. Perhaps you could drive your grandchildren to Sunday school or youth group if their parents work, or maybe you could invite your grandkids to your home for a weekly devotional time.

3. Make a plan to be organized and deliberate in making the most out of the time you have with your grandchildren. Teach them Bible stories, memorize Scripture together, have fun singing praise songs with them—these are all ways to "bring church to them" if they are part of a non-church-attending family.

Scriptures to Study

"Let us throw off everything that hinders and the sin that so easily entangles, and let us run with perseverance the race marked out for us" (Hebrews 12:1).

❖ We all have things—even good things—that can hinder and entangle us from running the race God has given us. What are these things in your life? Take a moment and ask God to help you identify them then make a plan for eliminating them so you can be free to serve Him as He desires.

"If you hold to my teaching, you are really my disciples. Then you will know the truth, and the truth will set you free" (John 8:31–32; see also Ephesians 4:15).

❖ The grandmother in this story spoke to her son about the biblical commandment of teaching our children about the Lord. As a result, God worked to free Todd's heart to serve Him once again, which resulted in his whole family returning to church. No matter how bound we may be, God's truth has power to free us.

"But I trust in you, O LORD; I say, 'You are my God.' My times are in your hands" (Psalm 31:14–15).

❖ One of the hardest things is to wait on God's timing. We are an impatient people who would much rather see God move in our timing. But His plans and ways are always perfect, and if we can just learn to trust in His timing, we will receive the best He has for us.

One Way to Pray

Lord, show me how I can come alongside my grandchildren's parents and effectively partner with them to raise my grandchild for You. Where my children have walked away from You or from church, I ask that You would use me to speak the right words to them to help bring them back. Touch my children's hearts so they would desire to do all they can to lead their children into a genuine relationship with You. I ask for creative ideas of how I can bring church to my grandchildren if necessary, so they can begin to have an understanding of Your love for them. And, help me to relax in Your perfect timing for my family, knowing that You are working in each of their hearts, and that our times are truly in Your loving hands. In Jesus' name. Amen.

Prayers, Notes, or Ideas

_____

_____

_____

_____

_____

_____

_____

CHAPTER 17

Jesus House
by Susan Lawrence

The impending birth of a grandchild should be cause for great joy and celebration. Our first grandchild arrived with a flurry of festivities. We attended showers, bought gifts, and readied our home for our new little visitor. When she finally arrived, we were ecstatic. Ben, our firstborn—our granddaughter's dad—had a wonderful job, while his wife, Nicole, planned on staying home to raise her daughter. Baby Bailey Ann lacked for nothing. Ben and Nicole were conscientious parents, reading to Bailey, providing her with play dates, and regularly taking her to church. We seized every opportunity to spend time with our precious granddaughter.

But when our nineteen-year-old adopted daughter, Teresa, had announced that she was pregnant with our second grandchild, it was not cause for celebration. Teresa had moved out of our home four months shy of her eighteenth birthday. She and her boyfriend, Andy, "couch surfed," sleeping in friends' living rooms and in shelters, begging odd jobs and money whenever and wherever they could. Neither had high school diplomas, and neither was employed. Both struggled with mental health issues, including bipolar disorder and depression. None of this provided a welcoming environment for a child.

Throughout her growing years, despite considerable conflict, we maintained a good relationship with our daughter. Teresa longed to know we loved her, and we affirmed that often, even in the depths of her rebellion. When she was in trouble, we were the first she would call.

As she shared the news of her pregnancy over the telephone, I could hear her sobs. "Teresa, it will be okay. We will help you. We'll figure out what's best," I said, trying to assure her as much as myself.

Even though I had difficulty believing what I said, I easily stepped into my usual role of soothing and calming Teresa. It was only after I hung up that I collapsed in tears. I knew in my head that all babies are created by God and that this baby was not an "accident." But in my heart I cried out, *How can this be good, or fair to a child?*

On Thanksgiving Day, Teresa and Andy came to my home for our traditional family gathering. When everyone else left, they stayed. Sitting on our couch, my husband and I shared our hearts with them, and they did the same with us.

"We think you should consider giving the baby up for adoption. Neither of you are in a position to be a good parent." My husband was gentle but firm, presenting what seemed to us to be the best solution. They were determined to be parents, however, and promised to find stable jobs and a place to live. They also knew they should be married, but the details of making their union legal were too difficult to handle immediately.

As my husband and I decorated the tree for Christmas, I hung a tiny white teddy bear on a branch. Though we were disappointed with Teresa and Andy's decision to keep the baby, and were concerned for this child, we knew that no situation was too hard for God. Standing next to the tree, my husband and I began to pray for this new little life.

We took both of them job hunting, even buying Andy something he never had—dress clothes for an interview. Our efforts paid off, and they were hired. Although the pay was minimal, it provided enough for rent on a studio apartment. They began attending church with us, and we praised God for the glimpses of maturity in their lives.

Then finally, the day came. "Mom, I think it's time. Can you meet us at the hospital?"

Cadence Rene entered the world on a sunny June afternoon. "Jesus loves you, this I know," I crooned softly to my newborn granddaughter. Her golden hair and petite features gave her the appearance of a fragile porcelain doll, and I knew an even more fragile spirit had been placed in my arms.

Teresa and Andy began bringing Cadence to church with them. When she was only a few weeks old, they dedicated her to the Lord before the congregation. "Lord, help me to do my part," I pledged, with the rest of the church, "to train Cadence to grow into a woman of faith."

We did our best to support Teresa and Andy without enabling them. But the new family lived in a precarious balance. Both parents had violent tempers, and, although they never harmed Cadence, they would often call our home late at night, screaming at each other and wanting us to intervene. Their jobs never lasted long, which often placed them in danger of eviction.

One day, in the midst of their chaos, I received a call from Teresa. "Mom …" she began, hesitantly, "we're having another baby." My heart fell. They were struggling so much already, how could they possibly handle two small children?

Once again, they asked for our help. We moved them into a new apartment, took Teresa to doctors' appointments, and continued teaching them parenting skills.

"You have a new baby grandson!" The memo came to me while I was teaching at school. Michail arrived on a February afternoon as snowflakes danced in the blustery wind. My husband had driven Teresa to the hospital, and then returned home with Cadence, watching her play until I arrived. After a quick supper, we all piled into the car and hurried back to the hospital where Cadence was introduced to her new brother.

Later that year, Teresa and Andy were married in a simple church wedding on a perfect, warm summer day. I had hoped this act of pledging faithfulness to each other before God would strengthen their marriage and commitment to their family. Parenting two small children, however, was more than Teresa could manage. Her frequent calls to Andy at work caused him to lose his job, and Teresa spiraled into depression, spending her days lying on the couch and leaving the care of the children to him.

Then, one day, we got a call from Andy. "Teresa's gone. I don't know where she is. She didn't leave a note, and she hasn't been home for two days."

She had returned to the pattern she'd begun as a teenager. Sometimes she would be gone for a day or two, sometimes up to a week. Shortly after Michail's first birthday, she left, and after a day or two, returned. When Andy refused to let her in the apartment, a violent confrontation ensued. The police arrived and enacted a restraining order, refusing her any contact with Andy.

The burden of raising the children fell completely on him, and he was ill equipped for the job. But he cared a great deal for the children, and he kept trying. My husband and I worked hard to establish a good relationship with him, and, rather than avoiding us, he sought our advice and support.

Living God's Presence Out Loud

In order to exude the presence of God, you must learn to live in the presence of God. Here are a few resources to help you do just that:

• *The Practice of the Presence of God* by Brother Lawrence

• *Having a Mary Heart in a Martha World* by Joanna Weaver

• *When You Can't Find God: How to Ignite the Power of His Presence* by Linda Evans Shepherd

• *When You Don't Know What to Pray: How to Talk to God about Anything* by Linda Evans Shepherd

We couldn't raise the children, even if Andy would relinquish them. Instead, we did what we could by pouring God's love into their lives every chance we got. When Cadence was four, I began taking her to our church's children's program on Wednesday nights. She was an avid learner, soaking in lessons about God like a little daisy in a summer rain. When we pulled into the church parking lot, she sighed contentedly, "We're home." Then she danced inside where she greeted everyone with a hug.

I taught her the songs I had learned as a child in Sunday school, and she sang her heart out to the Jesus she grew to love. I prayed with her, and then she would whisper her thoughts in simple child's language. "Thank You, Jesus, for my brother, my daddy, and my mommy. Amen." It didn't matter that we didn't know where Mommy was.

One evening, Cadence and her brother were spending the night at our house. We had just finished praying before the meal, and the "amens" had just been said. Cadence raised her eyes, looked quizzically around our dining room and asked, "Is this a Jesus house?"

Her question startled me, and I had to think before I answered. "Yes, Cadence, this is a Jesus house, because we love Jesus and try to live for Him."

"I always wanted to live in a Jesus house."

Again, I paused before answering. I knew she wasn't saying she wanted to live with me. Even though they lived in severe poverty and had an unstable home life, she loved her daddy dearly and wanted to be with him.

"Dear little Cadence," I finally responded. "You do live in a Jesus house! Wherever you are, Jesus is with you. Even when everything seems topsy-turvy, you live with Jesus, and He is bigger than any of your problems."

My explanation seemed to satisfy her, as a toothy grin lit up her face.

I can't give Cadence and Michail the family I think they deserve. I can't rescue them from poverty or prevent the myriad of other problems that their situation presents. But I can be the grandma who introduces them to Jesus, so they can live forever in a "Jesus house."

Grandparents in the Bible

Ahaz: Father of Hezekiah; Grandfather of Manasseh

When Hezekiah became king, he reopened and repaired the temple and removed the defilement (2 Chronicles 29:3, 5). With the northern kingdom, Israel, now exiled in Assyria, Hezekiah led the people of Judah in the south. They celebrated Passover for the first time since the kingdom divided two centuries earlier. In his later years, Hezekiah became prideful but repented. His son Manasseh succeeded him as king.

"Manasseh was twelve years old when he became king" and "he did evil in the eyes of the LORD" (2 Chronicles 33:1–2). He rebuilt the altars to foreign gods that his father, Hezekiah, had demolished (vs. 3–4). God brought the king of Assyria against Manasseh, and he was taken prisoner into Babylon (v. 11). Manasseh repented, and the Lord brought him back to Jerusalem. "Then Manasseh knew that the LORD is God" (vv. 12–13). Manasseh removed the altars from the temple and threw them out of the city (v. 15). His son Amon succeeded him as king.

Sandwiched between two evil kings is Hezekiah, who renewed the people's faith as he repaired God's temple. Hezekiah's son did evil but later repented, so God brought him back to Jerusalem—back to Himself. If you don't always like what you see in your grandchild, don't despair. God can restore anyone with a repentant heart. And even if a person isn't ready to repent, the Holy Spirit will never give up on him, and neither should you!

Points to Ponder

➤ Although the grandparents were disappointed in Teresa and Andy's choice to keep the baby, they still partnered with them in many ways. As Grandma put it, "We did our best to support [them] without enabling them." You may be in a situation with your child and grandchild that you're not happy about, but how can you show your support through partnership without enabling?

➤ Cadence's grandparents took a more active role with her once Teresa left. Although they didn't see her all the time, the little things they did—taking her to church, teaching her Christian songs, and teaching her to pray—turned into a big harvest as Cadence began to have a hunger for knowing Jesus. You may not be able to do a lot for your grandkids, but what little things can you do that have the potential for producing fruit in their lives?

➤ Grandma mentioned early on "we knew that no situation was too hard for God." But then she witnessed Teresa's abandonment of her family and Andy and Cadence living in poverty conditions. How can you continue to trust God and His promises when things seem to go from bad to worse? How can you encourage your family to have unwavering trust as well?

➤ Cadence recognized that her grandma lived in a Jesus house—not necessarily because of anything hanging on the walls, but because her grandmother carried the presence of God with her. In what ways do you carry God's presence in a recognizable way, especially around your grandkids? How can you teach your grandchildren that they can live in a Jesus house, too, regardless of the condition of their home life?

➤ Do you think the grandparents still wish Teresa and Andy would've given Cadence up for adoption? Why or why not? In what ways has God helped change your mind about things concerning your family that you were once set on? What does this say to you about God's wisdom versus ours?

Steps to Take

1. Whether you see your grandchildren frequently or not very often, little things you do for them spiritually can make a big difference in their lives. List some things you can start doing with your grandkids, such as teaching them songs, praying together at mealtime or bedtime, or buying them Christian DVDs, that will help plant seeds for an eternal harvest.

2. Think about people you've been around who always make you feel as though you're in a Jesus house when you're with them. What characteristics do these people have that you could begin to emulate?

3. Write down any issues where you currently need godly wisdom. Search out scriptures (Proverbs is a good place to start!) concerning wisdom, and begin to pray them aloud over your areas of concern. Be sure to listen for God's voice, and write down any thoughts He speaks to you.

Scriptures to Study

"How great is the love the Father has lavished on us, that we should be called children of God! And that is what we are!" (1 John 3:1).

❖ It can be hard to grasp that we are children of God, but it is true! The more your grandchildren can truly understand and receive this truth, the more they will see themselves as always being in a Jesus house, regardless of their circumstances.

"And I will ask the Father, and he will give you another Counselor to be with you forever—the Spirit of truth. The world cannot accept him, because it neither sees him nor knows him. But you know him, for he lives with you and will be in you" (John 14:16–17).

❖ How does it comfort you knowing that the Spirit of truth dwells in you and is always with you? How can you comfort your grandchildren with this same truth in a way they will understand?

"For the LORD gives wisdom, and from his mouth come knowledge and understanding. ... he guards the course of the just and protects the way of his faithful ones. Then you will

understand what is right and just and fair—every good path" (Proverbs 2:6, 8–9).

❖ When we seek godly wisdom, and not our own reasoning, we can trust that God Himself will protect our way. It may not seem like the right way at the time, but in time understanding will come.

One Way to Pray

Father God, I ask that You would help me to be such a godly example to my grandkids that they would sense Your presence when we're together. Help me to teach them, in a way that they'll understand, how they can always live in a Jesus house. Even when times get hard for my family, I know that You are with my grandchildren, guiding them and protecting them and drawing them to Yourself. Help me, Lord, to operate with godly wisdom concerning the decisions I need to make for my family so that not my will but Yours be done. In Jesus' name. Amen.

Prayers, Notes, or Ideas

Chapter 18

God and the Chickens
by Loritta Slayton

The hot summer sun shone down brightly on the old farmhouse, a testament of earlier days in the arid Colorado plains. A cracked brick patio rose and fell irregularly by the back entry from the growth of the giant oak tree shading it. Its shady boughs provided the perfect spot for the family to gather to escape the summer heat. The farmhouse needed much repair, but it still held an intrigue with its deteriorating veranda porch, two-storied gabled dormers, old wooden floors, and sculptured vents and hardware of days gone by. A couple of decrepit out-buildings were still standing, along with one small brick structure where the chickens roosted.

This farmhouse is where my grandson, Wesley, age ten; his sister, Kaileen, age nine; their brother, Dakota, age four; and Annabella, not yet three, lived with their mom and dad. Their mother's vegetable garden was well underway with summer growth, while the corn in the adjacent field stood tall with fresh stalks. In the sultry summer sun, the corn was nurtured by the cool waters streaming from the irrigation ditch.

Surrounding us, the rooster and his harem of chickens pecked contentedly. There was the chatter of other family members nearby, but Wesley and I were having a conversation all our own. We were talking about listening for God to speak to us. "Grandma," Wesley said, "I can't hear God speak to me." For a fleeting moment, my mind connected to another day, a little more than a year ago, when we had a similar conversation while sitting on the couch together.

Wesley's outbursts of anger resulted in the two of us being on the couch. When he got angry, I would be put to the test because I would become frustrated and angry as well. "What should I do, Lord?" I would ask again and again when I found myself in this situation. I soon learned that it was helpful to allow Wesley to sit on the couch for a moment while he calmed down, which in turn allowed me to calm down—and pray. After a while, I joined Wesley on the couch.

There on that old green couch, stained from children's dirty hands and numerous spills, and surrounded by toys and baby blankets, Wesley and I connected with God and each other. I realized Wesley needed to know how to hear God for himself. I began to share with Wesley from my own experiences. "Wesley, when you feel upset, stop a moment, and ask God what you should do. Listen quietly, and wait for Him to bring an idea or thought to your mind that will help you handle the situation better."

Wesley listened intently then responded, "Grandma, I can't hear God talk to me!" I knew he was really frustrated by this, so we continued talking about it, then I prayed with him. "Lord, please help Wesley learn to hear and recognize Your voice. Help him to make better choices. In Jesus' name, amen." I had to trust that in time, he would hear from God and learn how to be guided by His voice.

My grandchildren were going through a difficult time then, and I knew I needed to do all I could to help them stay close to God and not wander from their spiritual roots. It had become necessary for me to babysit my grandchildren while Wesley's mom was taking some classes to help their family gain better financial stability. Wesley's dad was in prison again, a pattern that had repeated itself as far back as Wesley could remember. Wesley struggled with anger and frustration over the habitual patterns of chaos and disappointment.

During this time of struggle for my grandkids, I'd been sitting on my own back patio, enjoying the warmth of the fall sun on my shoulders while spending time alone with the Lord. The Lord pointed out to me that praying for my grandchildren was no less important than praying for the adults. They, too, face the attacks of Satan as much as anyone. They needed to know how to fight in the spiritual realm just as the big folks do. I felt led to Mark 10:14—"allow the children to come to Me—do not forbid, or prevent, or hinder them" (AMP). I reflected on the word *hinder*.

> ### *Learning to Listen Activity*
>
> *Sit with your grandchildren in a noisy environment. Have them listen silently and intently for about two to three minutes to the various sounds around them. Then, choose three or four different sounds during that time and ask if they heard them. Now, choose one sound to have them listen for specifically. After a couple of minutes ask who heard it. God's voice is always easier to hear if we know what we're listening for!*

I realized that not only can we hinder them deliberately, but we can also hinder them by neglect. We can hinder children from coming to know God simply by not focusing on encouraging them to come to Him! As I started babysitting the children, I asked God to open up opportunities for me to talk with them about knowing Him.

The sun rose as I drove the half hour to my daughter's home twenty miles away. After a few minutes with my daughter, she left and it was my responsibility to get this little brood up and going. "Hello, Wesley, be sure and take your medicine right away ... Good morning, Kaileen, do you know what you're going to wear today? ... Just a minute Bella, Grandma will get you ... Okay, Dakota, let's get you something to eat ... Kaileen, can you grab the diaper wipes for me—we've got to get the babies changed and dressed."

One morning amidst all the rush, I glanced at the calendar on the dining room wall. There under the picture was a scripture: "In all your ways acknowledge him, and he will make your paths straight" (Proverbs 3:5–6 NASB). "Wesley," I said, "You know how Mom and Dad want you to answer 'Yes, Mom,' or 'Yes, Dad,' after they tell you to do something?"

Wesley nodded and said, "Uh-huh."

"Well," I continued, "that's how it is with God. When He tells us to do something, He wants us to say, 'Yes, God.' When we acknowledge Him, He can help us go in the right direction." With a quick prayer and hug, he was out the door to catch the bus.

By the time all the other kids were ready to go, we were often stressed and a bit emotional. There was no better remedy than to pray together. "Lord, we're upset right now. Help us to calm down and make better choices. Please forgive us and help us in forgiving one another."

As the kids and I drove down the road, we'd listen to a Christian radio station. One morning we heard the old hymn, "It Is Well with My Soul."

"Kaileen, do you know what that song means?"

"No," she replied.

Once again, a moment with God was available; an opportunity captured as I tried to help her understand the value of trusting God even when we can't understand what is happening.

I soon realized that the scripture I glanced at that one morning was also for Grandma. As I acknowledged God, recognizing Him in my current situation, He made my paths straight! He gave me His wisdom and allowed me to plant seeds of truth in my grandchildren for His kingdom.

So, at the old farmhouse that summer day, while talking about listening for God, I told Wesley, "When God speaks He doesn't sound like—'WESLEY, THIS IS GAAAWWWDDDD TALKING!'" I lowered my voice a couple of octaves and cupped my hands around my mouth to dramatize the sound. "Sometimes He brings a thought to you or sometimes put an impression on your heart; or it could be a scripture He brings to your mind that helps you."

Wesley was quiet for a moment, then his eyes grew big and he answered excitedly, "Well, Grandma, then I *have* heard God talk to me!" He continued, "The other day I thought about shooting one of Mom's chickens. Then two scriptures came to mind about how kids should obey their parents."

"That's good, Wesley!" I said. "That's exactly how God talks to us!"

There was more than chickens and corn growing out at the old farm. There was a young boy growing in his walk with God, along with a grandma who was growing right alongside him.

Grandparents in the Bible

Manasseh: Grandfather of Josiah

Manasseh's son, Amon, "did evil in the eyes of the LORD, as his father Manasseh had done … But unlike his father Manasseh, he did not humble himself before the LORD" (2 Chronicles 33:22–23). Amon's officials assassinated him, and his son, Josiah, was made king in his place.

"Josiah was eight years old when he became king … He did what was right in the eyes of the LORD … In the eighth year of his reign, while he was still young, he began to seek the God of his father David" (2 Chronicles 34:1–3). Josiah purged Judah and Jerusalem of idols and repaired God's temple. During this restoration, Hilkiah the priest found the Book of the Law of the Lord in the temple, which apparently had been lost for quite some time. The book was read to Josiah and he mourned. God was touched by Josiah's humility and promised not to bring punishment on Judah while he lived. Josiah had the Book read to all the people and directed them in pledging themselves to what the Book said, and, "As long as he lived, they did not fail to follow the LORD, the God of their fathers" (2 Chronicles 34:33).

Manasseh repented later in life, but his son did not learn from this. Amon did evil and did not repent. But Amon's son Josiah, although very young, sought God. Because of Josiah's leadership, the lost Word of God was found and the people followed God. Anyone, even a young child, who chooses to walk with God, can affect multitudes for His kingdom.

Points to Ponder

➢ There will always be moments of frustration and impatience in dealing with your grandkids. This grandmother gave herself a "time out" where she'd sit, calm down, and pray during such times. How do you handle these moments? If this method isn't working for you, what could you try instead?

➢ Grandma had good advice for Wesley when trying to help him hear from God when he was upset: "Stop a moment and ask God what you should do. Listen quietly, and wait for Him to bring an idea or thought to your mind that will help you handle the situation better." What advice or personal experiences can you share with your grandchildren to help them hear God's voice?

➢ We've all experienced some difficulty with not being able to hear from God. This can be especially trying for kids who don't yet know what God's voice sounds like. How have others helped you work through your frustration with this? How can you do the same for your grandkids?

➢ God showed this grandmother that "praying for [her] grandchildren was no less important than praying for the adults" because they also face Satan's attacks. In what ways do you think children are under spiritual attack even more than adults? How can you teach your grandchildren to fight effectively in the spirit realm?

➢ In what ways might you have hindered your grandchildren through neglect by not encouraging them to come to God? What steps can you take to remedy this? Take a moment to receive God's forgiveness for any way in which you may've hindered your grandkids. Ask God to show you specific ways you can encourage them to come to Him and listen for His voice.

Steps to Take

1. Devise an action plan for the next time you're caught in a moment of frustration, anger, or impatience with your grandkids. What can you do to ensure that you respond to them in a godly manner?

2. Think about how God speaks to you, how you know His voice, and any tests you apply to be certain it is His voice you're hearing. Prepare how you can share your own experiences and articulate to your grandchildren how they can learn to hear from God for themselves.

3. Arrange an opportunity to talk to your grandchildren about the spiritual battle we all face. Teach them from God's Word how they can be victorious in this battle. (See John 4:4; 5:3–5; Ephesians 6:10–18; James 4:7.)

Scriptures to Study

"Whether you turn to the right or to the left, your ears will hear a voice behind you, saying, 'This is the way; walk in it'" (Isaiah 30:21).

❖ Helping teach your grandkids how to hear God's voice is a great way to partner with their parents to influence them for the Lord. The sooner they can hear God's voice for themselves, the sooner God can guide their every step.

"I tell you the truth, the man who does not enter the sheep pen by the gate, but climbs in by some other way, is a thief and a robber. The man who enters by the gate is the shepherd of his sheep. … and the sheep listen to his voice. He calls his own sheep by name and leads them out. When he has brought out all his own, he goes on ahead of them, and his sheep follow him because they know his voice. But they will never follow a stranger; in fact, they will run away from him because they do not recognize a stranger's voice" (John 10:1–5).

❖ God promises that, as His children, we will know His voice and not follow a stranger's. Encourage your grandchildren to discuss with you the voices they hear inside them. You can help them discern the difference between God's voice,

Satan's voice, and their own voice as they're learning to recognize the voice of their Shepherd.

"Submit yourselves, then, to God. Resist the devil, and he will flee from you" (James 4:7).

❖ Kids need to know that in Christ they have the power to resist Satan for themselves. They should never fear our adversary as long as they are submitted to God.

One Way to Pray

Thank You, God, for the awesome privilege of hearing Your voice. Help my grandkids learn how to recognize Your voice when You speak to them. I pray they would always hear and obey Your will and never follow the voice of a stranger. Enable me to teach them how to hear from You and to encourage them when they get frustrated. Help me, too, to never hinder my grandkids from coming to You by neglecting to teach them all I can about You and Your ways. In Jesus' name. Amen.

Prayers, Notes, or Ideas

_____

_____

_____

_____

_____

_____

_____

_____

_____

_____

Chapter 19

Heart Talk
by Betty Johnson Dalrymple

Thunder roared and streaks of lightning flashed across the sky. *Oh no*, I thought as I stole a glance at my five-year-old grandson, Braxton. "This could be a very difficult trip home," I whispered as I peeked out the car window. It was springtime in the Rockies, and a typical afternoon rainstorm threatened. Braxton hated thunderstorms. In fact, Braxton was a fear-filled child.

It all began when he was just a baby and experienced several frightening episodes. As a newborn, Braxton needed surgery to cure a digestive problem. Then, six months later, he developed a respiratory problem and spent more time hospitalized. As his asthmatic condition worsened over the next few years, he was rushed to doctors' offices and hospitals several times. After each frightening experience, we noticed this little one becoming more and more fearful and hesitant to stray very far from his parents. My heart hurt for my grandson, and I wanted to relieve him of his fearful nature, reassure him that he was safe with me, and loved by God and his family.

"Will you babysit one day a week so I can help with our insurance business?" my daughter-in-law asked one day.

"I'd love to," I quickly responded, knowing this would give me a chance to spend more time with Braxton. *Maybe I can help him with his anxiety*, I thought.

One day as I sat down to rock my little grandson to sleep, I had an idea. I raised Braxton to my shoulder, leaned my mouth close to his ear, and began quietly singing a little tune: "God loves Braxton, Jesus loves Braxton, Mommy loves Braxton, Daddy loves Braxton, Nana loves Braxton …" and I continued naming each family member. Over and over, I repeated my little song until he was asleep, then I gently laid him in his crib. Each week, before naptime, I'd sing in his ear and pray that my fear-filled grandson would come to know he was loved by God, by Jesus, and by his whole family, and this love would push out his fear.

In my heart, I knew I was doing this because I understood fear and how it cripples a person, especially a young child or a teenager. I knew what it was like to grow up afraid of the dark, to fear the unknown, to feel helpless and homesick. I prayed this little boy would not have to experience the sadness and anxiety I'd known.

Later that year, Braxton began attending a Christian preschool. "I don't wanna stay here," he cried every day during that first week.

Each day when my son took Braxton to school, the teacher reassured him, "He'll be fine after you leave. He's just suffering from separation anxiety." On some days this was true. However, the crying and sadness occurred often enough to concern both his parents and his teachers.

One morning as I pulled into the church parking lot for a meeting, I noticed my son standing outside Braxton's classroom. "Is there a problem with Braxton?" I asked. "Why are you standing outside the door?"

"Braxton had a bad day yesterday so I thought I'd better stop by and make sure he's doing okay today," he answered. Then he asked me, "Do you have any suggestions, Mom?"

"I think the most important thing you can do is reassure him that he's loved," I said. "Since this is a Christian preschool, I believe both your and the teacher's reassurance that he's safe and loved by God and all of us will help him adjust." As the year passed, Braxton did adjust and began enjoying his time with his new friends.

Then he started kindergarten and once again anxiety, like an ugly thunderstorm, threatened on the horizon. Those first weeks of school were full of tears as big as raindrops. Making the adjustment was difficult.

When I heard the stories of Braxton's sadness, I remembered my own fear-filled days in first grade and the tears I'd shed because I didn't like leaving my safe haven at home. I wanted to help Braxton, and I asked God for guidance. "Please, Lord," I prayed.

> ## *An Encouraging Word*
>
> *" 'Train up a child in the way he should go, and when he is old he will not depart from it.' God said it and it will happen. Whether you're there to see it or not."*
>
> ("Touched by An Angel" flip calendar for August 7, c. 1997 CBS, Inc., printed by Garborg's)

"Show me how I can help this child understand that You are there with him, wanting him to feel comfortable and to enjoy school."

Now, on this babysitting afternoon, I listened to the rain on the car roof going "bam, bam, bam." It was deafening, and I heard my trying-to-be-brave five-year-old cry, "I'm scared, Nana," as he crouched against the car door. Tears glistened in his big brown eyes, and I understood his fear.

Swoosh! Swoosh! The windshield wipers fought to keep the pouring rain off the windshield, and I could barely see the road. *Crrraaaccckk!*

That one's close, I thought, and quickly swerved into a grocery store parking lot. I had to admit to myself that my little grandson was expressing outwardly what I was feeling inside.

I turned off the engine, slipped next to Braxton, and cuddled him close. "It's okay," I said. "Years ago, someone told me that the thunder and lightning won't hurt us while we're in the car. Let's believe that's true and talk about something fun. Remember," I added, "we know we're not alone because God is with us."

My reassuring comment regarding God's presence must have triggered something in Braxton's mind because he suddenly stopped crying and asked, "Nana, did you know that God talks to us in our hearts? We can't hear God like you and me talking right now," he said, pointing to his ears.

Then he moved away from me and began waving his outstretched arms in front of him, adding, "And He's not out here where you can see Him either. God talks to us here in our hearts," he said, pounding on his chest.

We both sat quietly, and after a few minutes of thoughtful silence, Braxton continued. "Does God talk to you like that, Nana?"

"Yes, often," I answered.

"Do you think He'll talk to me when I get big like you?" he continued.

"Oh, I'm sure He will," I answered.

"What do you think God will say to me?" Braxton asked, his eyes bright in anticipation.

I hesitated, then slowly leaned toward my little companion and whispered in his ear, "I think God will say, 'I love you, Braxton Wayne.'"

I'll never forget the smile that spread across my grandson's face. We'd both forgotten about the noisy thunder, the irritation of the swooshing windshield wipers, and the pounding rain on the roof. The inside of our car was completely filled with feelings of safety, comfort, and love.

Since that experience, when I recall that day, I always brush a tear from my eye because I knew then and I know now that my prayers for my fear-filled grandson were being answered. Was it the little tunes of love I'd sung in his ear when he was a baby? Was it the reassuring Bible verses he'd learned from his parents and preschool teachers? Whatever the earthly vehicle was, I knew the real source of reassurance came from God and was meant for both of us.

Slowly but surely, I've watched this once anxious little tot grow into a self-assured young man, still a bit cautious when faced with new situations, but willing to step out and give life a try, knowing that God continues talking to him in his heart.

Grandparents in the Bible

Josiah: Father of Jehoahaz and Jehoiakim; Grandfather of Jehoiachin

Josiah's son, Jehoahaz, became king, but Egypt's king dethroned him, making his brother, Eliakim, king and changing his name to Jehoiakim. Jehoiakim did evil in God's sight, and Nebuchadnezzar defeated him and deported him to Babylon. His son, Jehoiachin, succeeded Jehoiakim as king. Jehoiachin also did evil, and Nebuchadnezzar took him to Babylon, making his uncle, Zedekiah, king. Zedekiah also did evil in God's sight.

As the leaders and people of Israel became increasingly unfaithful to God, they defiled God's temple in Jerusalem. God brought Nebuchadnezzar to conquer them and carry them into exile in Babylon along with the articles from the temple. Nebuchadnezzar burned the temple to the ground and destroyed Jerusalem's protective wall. The people remained captive until the seventy years spoken by the prophet Jeremiah were fulfilled.

Then Cyrus, Persia's king, overpowered Babylon. God moved on his heart to rebuild the temple. Cyrus proclaimed that

God's people could return to rebuild the temple in Jerusalem (2 Chronicles 36).

After Josiah's godly influence ended, God's judgment came upon Judah. His judgment didn't destroy His legacy of faith but rather removed the evil leaders while preserving the bloodline from Abraham through David to Christ. Furthermore, the understanding about God was preserved in His Book, and the truth of God portrayed in the temple was no longer undermined by false worship. No matter how much evil reigns, God can preserve the legacy of faith handed down generation to generation.

Points to Ponder

> ➤ What are the different ways Grandma mentioned she prayed for Braxton? What did she pray for herself? How can you apply these prayers to your own situation?

> ➤ Consider this grandparent's response to Braxton's fears: She sang songs with a message of God's love. Braxton noted we can't hear God with our ears or see Him with our eyes, but He talks to us in our hearts. What songs can you sing, what prayers can you pray, or which reassuring Bible verses can you say over and over with your grandchildren until they sink through their ears and eyes into their hearts?

> ➤ This grandmother talked about her own battle with fear when she was growing up. What challenges or struggles did you experience during your childhood that you could share with your grandchildren that may help them? What insight did you gain from those struggles that they can also learn from?

> ➤ If your grandchild asked you what God might say if He talked to him or her, what would your answer be? How can you help your grandchildren to hear and recognize God's voice? Share one example with your grandkids of when you heard God speak to you.

➢ When her son asked for advice, Betty suggested he reinforce to Braxton that he was loved. How can you partner with your grandchildren's parents to help your grandchildren overcome the challenges they face?

Steps to Take

1. The unique challenge for Braxton in this story was fear. On paper, list your grandchildren by name. Beside each, list a unique challenge that grandchild faces. Then write a spiritual strength that might help this grandchild overcome each challenge: love; faith; mercy; forgiveness; self-control; patience; and so forth.

2. Find Bible stories and verses that can develop that spiritual characteristic in your grandchild, and share them with him or her. Begin to pray for this spiritual strength in your grandchild's life.

3. Find a science book, a museum, or a hymn that explores something wonderful in the world God created, such as thunderstorms or the hymn, "How Great Thou Art," which speaks of God's awesome wonder displayed in "rolling thunder." Make a date to explore God's wondrous world with your grandchild.

Scriptures to Study

"There is no fear in love. But perfect love drives out fear, because fear has to do with punishment. The one who fears is not made perfect in love" (1 John 4:18).

❖ What do you think "perfect love" is? Why do you think perfect love drives out fear? How can perfect love be applied to your family's situation?

"The fear of the LORD is the beginning of wisdom, and knowledge of the Holy One is understanding" (Proverbs 9:10; see also Psalm 111:10 and Proverbs 1:7).

❖ What is your understanding of the word *fear* in these verses? How can you help your grandchild understand the difference between this kind of "good" fear of the Lord and the kind of "bad" fear described in this chapter's story?

"The LORD himself goes before you and will be with you; he will never leave you nor forsake you. Do not be afraid; do not be discouraged" (Deuteronomy 31:8).

❖ Share this word of hope with your grandchild. God is always with us and will never, ever leave us! Whether it's starting a new year at school or sitting in a car in a thunderstorm, your grandchild can be assured that God will be with him, protecting and comforting him.

One Way to Pray

*Dear Lord, You know each of my grandchildren far better than I do.
Give me insight into what each is struggling with. Then give me
wisdom to find a way to help them grow through that challenge in
their faith, knowledge, and understanding of You. And where there
are hardships or struggles they're facing that I cannot see,
supernaturally enable me to teach them the perfect truth they need to
know to walk through that struggle and remain faithful to You.
Teach me how to love each of them with Your perfect love so they
will never fear coming to me for help. In Jesus' name. Amen.*

Prayers, Notes, or Ideas

_____

_____

_____

_____

_____

_____

_____

_____

_____

Chapter 20

Jack's Fear
by Ann Kronwald

"Protect me, Nana! They're getting closer."

Jack's little body was visibly shaking and plastered so tightly against my side we were practically one. His siblings, as always, followed suit. One burrowed into my arms burying his head in my neck. The other hung off my back crying while trying to balance on the bench where we sat.

I have to admit, I bit my lip and turned my head more than once to stifle my amusement. After all, here we were in the happiest of all places on earth—the petting zoo—where gleeful children ran with abandon from one old sleeping goat to the next to brush, poke, pull, hug, and generally torment these mellow creatures. And there in the midst of all the excitement, we sat in our own little nightmare, huddled on top of each other on a bench in the corner. All of the coaxing in the world wasn't about to pry an inch of breathing room between our bodies, so we left on a quest for a less dangerous adventure.

Welcome to three-month *toddler duty!* With my daughter-in-law on bed-rest, I was now experiencing Jack's fears on a regular basis. Even a neighbor's routine dog walk—on a leash and way across the boulevard—caused Jack to quickly move behind me and beg for safety. But his fears were not limited to animals. Every plumber, tree-trimmer, and trash collector was scrutinized by Jack. "Is he a good man or a bad man, Nana?" He had to know.

Being the firstborn of all the grandkids, it was Jack's unfortunate job to blaze the trail. The others watched him meticulously. If he had tested something and found it to be safe, they would all jump in with abandon. But Jack had no front man to test his world for him, and he always tested new waters by sticking his toe in the shallow end, never diving into the deep end. So his risk-taking was a very slow process. But I understood; this Nana has enough fears of her own to be able to relate to the Jacks of the world.

My son and daughter-in-law had been giving their children an excellent picture of a huge and loving God, who was definitely big enough to protect them. Over time, Jack had finally come to start relying on this huge God. I knew that in my three months of child care, it was my job not to mess up that foundation, but rather to build on it.

During this same time period, I happened to be teaching a course on the names of God to women at our church. Two of those names in particular helped Jack and me through our days. *El Shaddai* is the Almighty God who is strong and strengthens us despite our many weaknesses.

"Hey, Jack," I said one day, "One of God's names means 'Almighty.' What kinds of things do you think God is mightier than?"

Jack thought about my question for a few seconds then blurted out, "Mean dogs!"

"Yes, definitely," I said, encouraging him. "And how about lightning? Do you think He could handle lightning?"

"I think so," said Jack.

Back and forth we went, coming up with as many things as possible that God was stronger than. This became a regular game for the two of us, with each trying to outdo the other.

God's Many Names

God has many different names that reveal His character in various ways. The more we know about who God really is, the more we can trust Him in any of our situations.

- El Olam (The Everlasting God; Isaiah 40:28–31)
- El Shaddai (Lord God Almighty; Genesis 17:1)
- El Elyon (The Most High God; Isaiah 14:13–14)
- Jehovah-Jireh (The Lord Will Provide; Genesis 22:14)
- Jehovah-Nissi (The Lord My Banner; Exodus 17:15)
- Jehovah-Rapha (The Lord Our Healer; Exodus 15:26)
- Jehovah-Rohi (The Lord Our Shepherd; Psalm 23:1)
- Jehovah-Shalom (The Lord Is Peace; Judges 6:24)
- Jehovah-Shammah (The Lord Is There; Ezekiel 48:35)
- Jehovah-Tsidkenu (The Lord Our Righteousness; Jeremiah 23:6)

Our day always ended with a drive to Dad's office to send the kids home. During that drive, Jack and I began memorizing the lyrics to the song "You Are Stronger." It was simply awesome for me to hear my four-year-old-grandson singing about the power of the Resurrection. And we used the chorus back at home to add to our ever-growing list of things that God was stronger than.

The other name I had been studying and found useful in my times with Jack was *Jehovah-Shalom*. This describes God as the one who replaces our fears with His peace—not necessarily by removing us *out* of our circumstances, but by being present with us *in* our circumstances. I prayed that Jack was not only seeing a bigger, stronger God, but one who was near enough to be in his frightening situations with him.

Jack and I had conversations about this aspect of God as well. He understood that God could be everywhere, so I helped him conclude that it was possible for God to be with every person in the world who happened to be afraid. He never had to feel alone in his fears. Not only would God be with him, but He would give him the peace to get through those scary times.

I realized during story time one day that our conversations about *Jehovah-Shalom* had borne fruit. It was my practice to tell my grandkids stories before naptime. Sometimes these stories were based on my life growing up on a farm, or my adventures in other countries, or sometimes they were merely the product of my imagination at that moment. (Those were the ones that always stumped me when I was asked to retell them the next day.)

During one of these imaginary stories, I added the drama "… and I was so afraid." A little four-year-old voice interrupted, "But Nana, God would be *with* you!" I rejoiced at what his young brain had grasped. His little heart had embraced *Jehovah-Shalom* as an obvious answer for my dilemma. I was excited to know that he was "getting it."

So it went for three months. Jack even overwhelmed both of us one day as he chose to greet and make conversation with our local trash collector. "Hi, my name's Jack," he began, when the man jumped out of the truck to take our garbage bags. The man introduced himself and asked Jack how he was doing. "I'm good," was the reply. Jack walked back up our driveway, his chest puffed out with pride.

During my final week of toddler duty, the kids and I made our last trip to the zoo. Jack announced that he intended to pet the goats. I applauded his courage but knew there was still a lot of time to weasel out of this plan, especially since it was formed before we had even reached the zoo parking lot. After we arrived and walked closer to the dreaded danger zone, Jack thought it necessary to qualify his previous statement. "I didn't say I *would*, I said I *might* pet the goats." I didn't respond and quickly found interest in something in the other direction to disguise my lack of concern over his very serious wavering.

But did you know that the mighty *El Shaddai* is even stronger than a fear of old goats, and that *Jehovah-Shalom* can accompany you right into the ominous petting zoo? That's right, once-fearful Jack walked directly through the gate, picked out a special brush, and began to gently run it down an old nanny's bristly back. Though Jack was a bit jittery, he stayed true to his task and worked with great concentration. Each of his siblings cautiously watched, then did the same.

On our drive to his dad's office that evening, we talked about the zoo. And then, of course, came the familiar request, "Play number eight, Nana." Our day had brought special meaning to "You Are Stronger." With great pleasure, I joined in with the mousy high voices already in full swing and helped praise the God who is stronger than any of our fears. Jack and I have learned, each in our own way, that God "gives strength to the weary and increases the power of the weak" (Isaiah 40:29).

Grandparents in the Bible

Shealtiel: Grandfather of Zerubbabel

Few of God's people wished to return to Israel after seventy years in Babylon. A faithful group returned under the leadership of Ezra, Nehemiah, and Zerubbabel. Even with these few, God continued the royal bloodline of His promise from Abraham through David to the Messiah.

Jehoiachin's son, Shealtiel, continued David's royal line to his son, Pedaiah, and to Pedaiah's son Zerubbabel. To the prophet Zecharaiah, God said these familiar sayings regarding not only the rebuilding of the temple, but the continuing building to the Person Messiah:

"This is the word of the LORD to Zerubbabel: 'Not by might nor by power, but by my Spirit,' says the LORD Almighty … 'The hands of Zerubbabel have laid the foundation of this temple; his hands will also complete it …

"'Who despises the day of small things? Men will rejoice when they see the plumb line in the hand of Zerubbabel'" (Zechariah 4:6, 9–10).

Matthew and Luke trace the remaining royal bloodline to Jesus in their (sometimes abbreviated) genealogies filled with relatively unknown names. Matthew traces the bloodline from Zerubbabel to Joseph and Mary and then to Jesus in 1:13–16. Luke traces the bloodline in the other direction, from Jesus through Mary and Joseph back to Zerubbabel in 3:23–27.

Through both evil and good parents and grandparents, God is able to accomplish His plan and continue the legacy of faith, which is the knowledge of Him, from generation to generation. Where do you fit into God's plan for the future generations of your family?

Points to Ponder

> ➤ The grandchildren in this story had parents who were raising them in the things of the Lord. Grandma saw her role as helping the parents build on the foundation they had already laid in the kids' lives. What spiritual foundations are you able to build on as a result of your grandchild's parents? What spiritual foundations do you believe you need to lay yourself? How can you partner with your children to do this?

> ➤ What fears, insecurities, or difficult emotions does your grandchild struggle with? In what spiritual and practical ways can you come alongside her parents to help her gain victory in these areas? What personal experiences could you share with your grandchild to help her?

> ➤ How have you been comforted in the past as you've learned about God's character through His various names? What fun and creative methods can you use to teach your grandchild about the meaning of God's names and what they reveal about Him?

> ➤ This grandmother had a practice of telling her grandkids stories before naptime. Do you have a regular activity or special time with your grandkids? If so, what stories or object lessons could you incorporate into this time that demonstrate

God's greatness or awesome love that drives out all fear? If you don't, what special activity could you begin doing with them on a regular basis?

➤ In what everyday ways can you begin to reveal God's power and majesty to your grandchildren that will help them have a greater faith for His ability to keep them safe and secure?

Steps to Take

1. Look up the various names of God (see "God's Many Names" in this chapter) with your grandchild. Find out who she most needs God to be for her right now. Invite God into her situation using His corresponding name, thanking Him for being everything we need Him to be.

2. Create your own game with your grandchild similar to what this grandma did. Rehearse with your grandchild who or what God is stronger than, bigger than, smarter than, and so forth, depending on what fears or insecurities she faces.

3. Work with your grandchild on one particular fear or concern she has. Together, find scriptures that address God's ability to conquer this fear. Pray for her in this area then put feet to your faith by helping your grandchild overcome her fear in practical ways.

Scriptures to Study

"I will fear no evil, for you are with me; your rod and your staff, they comfort me" (Psalm 23:4).

❖ When we truly understand that God is always with us and that we can trust Him, we will no longer have anything to fear. Take time to help your grandchild get to know God intimately and learn to trust Him at all times.

"I pray that out of his glorious riches he may strengthen you with power through his Spirit in your inner being, so that Christ may dwell in your hearts through faith. And I pray that you, being rooted and established in love, may have power, together with all the saints, to grasp how wide and long and high and deep is the love of Christ, and to know this love that surpasses knowledge—that you may be filled to the measure of all the fullness of God" (Ephesians 3:16–19).

❖ What a power prayer to pray over your grandchild! Personalize this prayer using your grandchild's name, and watch God fill her with a revelation of His love, which in turn will drive out her fears.

"Neither death nor life, neither angels nor demons, neither the present nor the future, nor any powers, neither height nor depth, nor anything else in all creation, will be able to separate us from

the love of God that is in Christ Jesus our Lord" (Romans 8:38–39).

❖ Even if the whole world crumbles around us, God's love for us will remain. There is no stronger force in the universe than the love of God. Encourage your grandchild regularly by reminding her how much God loves her.

One Way to Pray

Most High God, thank You for revealing Yourself to Your people through Your Word and through Your names. You are truly all we need in every circumstance of our lives. I ask that You would help me to effectively partner with my grandchild's parents to continue building upon the spiritual foundation in my grandchild's life. Where there are fears or insecurities, give me wisdom to know how to help my grandchild overcome them by trusting in You and Your love for her. Reveal Yourself now to my grandchild in whatever way she needs You most. In Jesus' name. Amen.

Prayers, Notes, or Ideas

_____

_____

_____

_____

_____

_____

_____

_____

_____

Your Role as Grandparent

Have we touched on your grandparenting obstacles? Did one of the stories you just read come close to your situation? Or did we hit the nail on the head and you saw yourself and your grandparenting challenges in this book? Maybe your story is completely unrelated to any of these stories or the challenges these grandparents described and you're struggling with something completely unique.

Whatever the case, we all have one thing in common: the God of all is with us. He knows what to do in your situation. He can lead you. He can intervene. Ultimately, it is up to Him to draw hearts and minds to Himself—including the hearts and minds of your grandchildren and children.

We live in a time of extraordinary circumstances and events. We all— our society, our nation, our world—need grandparents actively influencing their grandchildren for Christ. We need to be intentional. It takes effort. It takes prayer. It takes you.

Through the twenty stories and the side articles, resources, and other materials in this book, we hope you found ideas and inspiration that will help you reach *your* grandchildren for Christ.

Your role as a grandparent in the lives of your grandchildren is unique and powerful. Your influence is incredibly important. No one else has the power or the influence that you do in the lives of the young people in your life.

Never forget that no matter who you are or what your situation is, God is in it with you. He has the power to make your efforts for His kingdom take root and bear fruit. He just needs you to stay involved. Show up. Be there. Stay in the game. Or get in the fight. Then watch what God does through you to reach your grandchild for Him.

May God richly bless your efforts for Him and His kingdom, and may you see the results of your efforts and the answers to your most fervent prayers both in this life, and in the next.

You are in our prayers,

Renée and Dianne

End Notes

Introduction

1. eds., "Surprising Facts about Grandparents," Grandparents.com, August 12, 2009, http://bit.ly/KtbPEB.

2. "A New Generation Expresses Its Skepticism and Frustration with Christianity," *The Barna Update*, August 24, 2007.

3. Thom S. Rainer, *The Bridger Generation* (Nashville, TN: Broadman & Holman, 2006).

4. "Barna Survey Examines Changes in Worldview Among Christians over the Past 13 Years," *The Barna Update*, March 6, 2009.

5. "A New Generation Expresses Its Skepticism and Frustration with Christianity," Barna Group, www.Barna.org, September 24, 2007, http://bit.ly/LfrIhO.

(ED. NOTE: The shortened links above provide direct access to the articles at the time of publication. Readers may also access the articles by searching the article title on the main website reference provided in the citation.)

Contributor Bios (alphabetized)

Barbara Baranowski is a writer and inspirational speaker devoted to family, educational, and spiritual issues. She lives with her husband, John, in Richmond, Virginia, where she retired as a middle school teacher. She and John enjoy their two daughters, sons-in-law, and five grandchildren. She believes grandparenting is her high calling at this time in her life. She enjoys traveling with family, and her new book, *In God's Creation: Devotions for the Outdoors* seeks to daily bring its readers closer to God.

Elaine Burbridge grew up in a small Texas town where storytelling was an everyday occurrence in her family. Her dream of writing started when she accepted a position as society editor in the town's newspaper. The newspaper didn't make it, but Elaine's dream to write did. She loves being a grandmother and writing about her grandchildren. Elaine resides in Richardson, Texas.

Christina Carmichael has approximately 375 articles and short stories. She has recently remarried after several years as a widow when her first husband, who was disabled for 22 years, passed away. She is enjoying her new marriage and her many trips together with her husband.

Peggy Cunningham and her husband have served as missionaries since 1981 in Bolivia, South America, where they have a children's ministry and two churches. She has written 13 children's books and contributes to Devokids.com, *The Voice of Grace and Truth,* and various other Christian publications. You can learn more about Peggy at www.peggyjcunningham.com.

Annalee Davis and her husband, Joel, live in Hillsborough, New Jersey. Annalee is an ordained minister, conference and retreat speaker, author, harpist, and adjunct professor. She can be reached at reverendannalee@comcast.net.

Elsi Dodge is a single, retired teacher of special needs children. Living in Boulder, Colorado, she travels in a 30-foot RV with the dubious assistance of her beagle and a small saber-toothed tiger, cleverly disguised as a tabby cat. In her spare time she tutors, sings in a choir, co-leads a Bible study, works with a church youth group, and (obviously) writes. You can find her blogging at www.RVTourist.com/blog.

Lea Dory has been published in magazines for both children and adults. A broad range of personal experiences has provided plenty of material for her lifelong passion for writing. But, her greatest joy and satisfaction comes from spending time with her grandchildren.

Francine Duckworth was born in Needles, California, and during her childhood, her father worked for the Santa Fe Railroad. Francine lived in a boxcar until their family moved to the Los Angeles area! At 16 she felt God's call on her life to be a missionary. It took 17 years, but at the age of 33, Francine and her family moved to the South Pacific where they were missionaries for the Church of the Nazarene for 20 years. Currently a pastor's wife in Brush, Colorado, she taught special education for several years after returning from Samoa.

Paula Freeman is the founder and executive director of Hope's Promise adoption and orphan care ministry (www.hopespromise.com). She and her husband, Ray, delight in their family and live in breathtaking Colorado.

Grace Hewson taught creative writing to homeschooled teens before deciding to try her hand at writing professionally. She is the author of *Rise from the Ashes,* a speculative fiction trilogy dealing with spiritual warfare. She also hosts an inspirational blog and shares her faith by producing multi-media messages to air on Youtube. Grace enjoys riding her Harley across the country and vacationing with her seven grandchildren.

Betty Johnson Dalrymple, a freelance writer of inspirational devotions and articles, has contributed to numerous popular devotional books. She enjoys traveling, playing golf, and spending time with her husband and their large blended family, including 19 grandchildren!

Ann Kronwald writes and teaches women's Bible studies in Chandler, Arizona, where she lives and works with her husband, David. They have four grown children and seven grandchildren. Ann enjoys writing about the names of God at www.HisNameMyPurpose.com.

Susan Lawrence is a Christian author, speaker, and storyteller. She has authored two published devotional books (*A Family Garden of Christian Virtues* and *A Young Child's Garden of Christian Virtues*) and has been a contributing author to many others. She lives with her husband and her yellow Lab, Annie, in a little house in the woods.

Lynn Leissler lives in a small town in Oregon, her days filled with family and friends, writing, quilting, gardening, and traveling. Kris Kringle, her cat, perches on a windowsill as she pens her monthly column in *The Christian Journal* and works on *The Fix-It Sisters*, a cozy mystery.

Kathie Mitchell and her husband, Mike, live in Milton, Pennsylvania. They have two married children and four grandsons. Kathie is a special-needs job coach. She enjoys writing and playing cornet in the Repasz Community Band.

Abigail Paul lives with her husband in the good ole USA. They enjoying walking the neighborhood, traveling any chance they get, and hanging out with their children. They enjoy marriage and family as God's greatest blessings, second only to relationship with Jesus Christ.

Rhonda Rivers never had a relationship with her grandparents. Her grandchildren are most precious to her, and her prayer is that God would direct any influence she might have on them. Remembering that Jesus has such a heart for children, she prays for their salvation in their youth so they may experience life abundantly.

Loritta Slayton has a passion for the Lord and His Word. She loves to share how Scripture has been the light on her path and God's love and faithfulness, her strong hope and victory. Learning to know God through the trials of life have made her who she is today.

Marilyn Stouter was arrested by God in 1983 when, through dreams, He encouraged and prepared her for future events. One such dream prepared her for a daughter's marriage and move overseas. After retiring from a high-tech management position, Marilyn now enjoys each summer as her two daughters, their husbands, and three grandchildren all gather together. Her passion is to see the Church become what God intended it to be; to reveal a God of greatness and power with His people walking in victory.

Kristin Lee Taylor lives in Southern California with her husband. She has five kids and twelve grandkids. She has authored thirty books and enjoys camping with her grandkids, attending plays, and gardening.

About the Authors

Dianne E. Butts is a freelance writer, author, and screenwriter. Her latest book, *Deliver Me* (www.DeliverMeBook.com), for those in an unplanned pregnancy or with one in their past, is a Christian Small Publishers Association "Book of the Year" award winner and inspired her first short film: http://bit.ly/TheChoiceFilm. She has over 300 articles published in Christian magazines and websites, and has contributed to nineteen books. She writes frequently for www.FindingGodDaily.com, www.TheChristianPulse.com, and www.ThinkingAboutSuicide.com. Her first book, *Dear America*, is now available on Kindle. She enjoys riding motorcycles with her husband, Hal, and gardening with her cat, PC. They live in Colorado.

Visit Dianne's website: www.dianneebutts.com

Renée Gray-Wilburn is the author of nearly 200 published pieces, including dozens of magazine articles, two children's books (*Volcanoes* and *Earthquakes*, Capstone Press), contributions to several compilation books, including the *Cup of Comfort* series and *Life Savors for Women*, and over a dozen children's curriculum books. Renée has a passion for instilling biblical truths into the hearts of children and loves helping others through her writing to do the same. She makes her home in Colorado Springs with her husband, Derrick, and their three children, Conner, Cayla, and Chandler.

Visit Renée's website: www.awaywithwordswriting.wordpress.com

Visit the
Grandparenting Through Obstacles
website, too!
http://grandparentingthruobstacles.wordpress.com/

Resources

Staying Connected over the Miles:
Facebook (www.facebook.com), Chapter 2
MySpace (www.myspace.com), Chapter 2
Skype (www.skype.com), Chapter 8
Twitter (www.twitter.com), Chapter 2

Bible Studies and Events for Kids:
AWANA (www.awana.org), Chapter 16
Backyard Bible Club
(www.childrendesiringgod.org/curriculum/), Chapter 4
Bible Study Fellowship International
(www.bsfinternational.org), Chapter 4, 14
MOPS (www.mops.org), Chapter 4

Biblically Centered Vacations:
Alpha Omega Institute (www.discovercreation.org),
Chapter 7
Ark Encounter (www.arkencounter.com), Chapter 7
Creation Museum (www.creationmuseum.org), Chapter 7
The Holy Land Experience (www.holylandexperience.com),
Chapter 7

Entertainment Industry Ministries:
168 Project (www.168project.com), Chapter 9
Act One (www.ActOneProgram.com), Chapter 9
Arts and Entertainment Ministries (www.A-E-M.org),
Chapter 9
Hollywood Prayer Network
(www.HollywoodPrayerNetwork.org), Chapter 9
Movie Guide (www.MovieGuide.org), Chapter 9

At-Home Missionary / Outreach Ideas:
Angel Tree (www.angeltree.org), Chapter 10
Compassion International (www.compassion.com),
Chapter 10
Open Doors (www.opendoors.org), Chapter 10

Open Doors in the USA (www.opendoorsusa.org),
Chapter 10
Operation Christmas Child (www.samaritanspurse.org),
Chapter 10
Voice of the Martyrs (www.persecution.com), Chapter 10
World Vision (www.worldvision.org), Chapter 10

Armor of God Children's Resources:
Armor of God coloring book with stickers (Standard
Publishing), Chapter 13
"Full Armor of God" game (ages 4-8, David C. Cook
Ministries), Chapter 13
Full Armor of God costume (David C. Cook Ministries),
Chapter 13
*The Armor of God: A Children's Bible Study in Ephesians
6:10–18*—Paperback by David Walters, Chapter 13

For Parents of Christian Teens:
*Already Gone: Why Your Kids Will Quit Church and What
You Can Do to Stop It* by Ken Ham and Britt Beemer,
Chapter 9

Resources for Living in God's Presence:
Having a Mary Heart in a Martha World by Joanna Weaver,
Chapter 17
The Practice of the Presence of God by Brother Lawrence,
Chapter 17
*When You Can't Find God: How to Ignite the Power of His
Presence* by Linda Evans Shepherd, Chapter 17
*When You Don't Know What to Pray: How to Talk to God
about Anything* by Linda Evans Shepherd, Chapter 17

Look for other books
published by

Pix-N-Pens Publishing

www.PixNPens.com

and

www.WriteIntegrity.com

Made in the USA
Charleston, SC
20 August 2012